How Do You Know That's a Tooth?

Lloyd Mattson

About The Cover

God gave us two books: the Bible and the creation. Both speak of God's power, grace, and glory. The cover photo unites the two. Wooly mammoth fossils Roger Green dug from his Alaska gold mine frame my father's old Bible. The tooth that gave the book its name anchors the lower right corner.

Photograph by Keith Mattson.

How Do You Know That's a Tooth?

Nearing the Summit

Lloyd Mattson

Wordshed Books
Duluth, Minnesota

How Do You Know That's a Tooth?

For additional copies and information on
Wordshed eBooks, contact:
Lloyd Mattson
127 E Calvary Road #301,
Duluth Minnesota 55803
218-409-9034
mattson.lloyd1@gmail.com.

ISBN: 0-942684-15-X

Published by Wordshed Books
Printed by Arrow Printing, Bemidji, Minnesota

Dedication
To the memory of my Elsie and the
family she gave me.

Keith, Kevin, Sally David, Elsie, Joel (circa 1963)

Joel, Sally, Lloyd, Elsie, Kevin, Keith, David at
Lloyd's and Elsie's 66th Wedding Anniversary.

Acknowledgements

Thanks to

- Sally Rogers for a final read-through.
- Keith Mattson for cover and text photographs.
- Kevin Mattson for design and type setting.
- Dave and Joel Mattson for stories.
- Bob Kelly for the Foreword and Part Three, Hole News quotes.
- A special friend whose insights and labors vastly improved the book.

Table of Contents

Books by Lloyd Mattson

Memoir series:
All the Days of My Life
Never Baptize Downstream
By the Campfire's Ruddy Glow (eBook)
The Great Land (eBook)
The Making of Many Books (eBook)
How Do You Know That's a Tooth?

Wordshed Mission books:
ALASKA: New Life for an Ancient People
ALASKA: A Man from Kanatak (with Paul Boskoffsky)
Bigfoot and the Michigamme Trolls
What is God Like? (with Len Carlson)
Watch Night
MANpower

The Making of Many Books (eBook) contains a full listing of Lloyd's writings.

Foreword
Bob Kelly

"...the pleasantness of one's friend springs from his earnest counsel."
(Proverbs 27: 9b, NIV)
"...a man's counsel is sweet to his friend."
(Proverbs 27:9b, NASB)
"...a sweet friendship refreshes the soul."
(Proverbs 27:9b, The Message)

It's been only a few years since Lloyd Mattson first entered my life but his friendship has been refreshing my soul regularly ever since. It was a mutual friend who first suggested that I might enjoy *The Hole News*, Lloyd's nightly recollections and reminiscences, which he's been writing in the predawn hours after his wife Elsie had been called home. He described those hours as his "hole in the night," and began passing his thoughts on, first to a few family members and close friends.

Recognizing the wisdom each edition of *The Hole News* contained, those few began sharing it with others. So it was that in April 2010, an issue first arrived in my inbox. I was immediately hooked and today, four years later, more than five hundred issues reside in my "Mattson" email folder. Not only are they chock-full of wisdom, but he writes in a style that's wonderfully expressive, reasonable and readable.

Consider these words from one of the first issues I received: "I welcome benign dialogue on any questions these spontaneous perambulations may raise. I have no agenda. I am an old-earth creationist, a position reached after years of Bible study, observing, and pondering, but I can always use new light. . . . The risen Savior, Jesus—true God and true man—is the core of the gospel. In Him we live and move and have our being. I am brother to all who hold that truth and a friend to all others."

As a writer and editor myself, I've had a life-long love affair with words and, for the past 30-plus years, have been an avid collector of the wit and wisdom of others. I add to this collection of quotations almost daily, so it will come as no surprise that I regularly harvest selections from *The Hole News*.

Lloyd writes a lot about friendship. Consider these words: "We need friends as much as we need food, shelter, and clothing. Friends are a necessity of life. When you find yourself running low, plug into an old or new friendship. You'll get a real charge."

He and I have spent a mere handful of hours together, but I've been richly and continually blessed by our friendship. I predict that you won't get very far into the pages that follow before you begin to feel the same way.

Prologue

Lloyd Mattson

This wrap-up of the memoir series will be my last print book. E-books will follow as my wits and years allow. *How Do You Know That's a Tooth?* blends new and old writings, some written by family. Part One contains entries that will persuade some readers I have strayed from the faith. I have outgrown some teachings from my youth.

Am I rock-solid certain my current views are final truth? Certainly not. Beware of anyone who takes that stance.

Part Two gleans writings from years past.

Part Three came from a friend, Quotemeister Bob Kelly. The book's title was the gift of an angry woman at a church picnic. Here's the story.

I was preaching for our vacationing pastor and I invited the kids to the platform for a story before they escaped to children's church. My prop was a black, gnarled, wooly mammoth tooth dug from an Alaska gold mine by my friend Roger Green. The kids passed the heavy fossil around the circle as I told about animals that once roamed North America. I concluded the story by saying, "The critter that owned this tooth died about 16,000 years ago."

That lit a brush fire. A knot of young-earth creationists caucused. Convinced that God created the entire universe in six 24-hour days six to ten-thousand years ago, nothing could be 16,000 years old. Mattson was teaching heresy.

Unaware of the fire, and thinking older folks might find the fossil interesting, I took it to the picnic and placed it near the watermelon. I stood nearby to answer questions. Not a soul came. Finally, an older woman approached, seeking watermelon. I said, "What do you think of my tooth?" In a voice dripping vinegar she replied, *"How do you know that's a tooth?"*

That set me thinking. How do I know anything? Dare the likes of me question teachings set forth by recent Church Fathers? What led me to abandon teachings of my youth? Does paleontology contradict Genesis? This book probes these and other questions. I lean on George Rawson's 1835 hymn poem:

We limit not the truth of God
To our poor reach of mind,
By notions of our day and sect,
Crude, partial and confined.
Now let a new and better hope
Within our hearts be stirred:
The Lord hath yet more light and truth
To break forth from His Word.

Part One

Part One contains reflections, speculations, and stories that range far and wide, many adapted from my Hole News blog. Some entries probe murky waters, where one person's orthodoxy is another person's heresy.

Mystery is a recurring theme for God's ways are not our ways. My entries state what I believe, but I mount no defense when I depart from tradition. I welcome new light based on sound reason, but I am not interested in rehashing old debates.

I follow Bible translators in the use of pronouns referring to deity.

My Creed

I believe God revealed his truth to mankind on two levels: the Bible and his other book, the creation. I firmly believe the Bible as God gave it, but I don't believe every Bible interpretation.

I believe in Mystery, the overarching factor in all spiritual inquiry. There is far more we can't know about God and his ways than we can know.

I believe in the Incarnation. God became man to teach by precept and example all the human mind can grasp of eternal truths. Jesus, not the Bible, is the ultimate authority. He is not subject to interpretation.

I believe in the Atonement: the cross, the empty tomb, the resurrection, and the ascension.

I believe in the kingdom, the sphere where the King reigns. The King holds all power and fulfills his purpose through his followers in everyday living. Life knows no secular moments.

I believe in the Consummation. History continually moves toward a new heaven and earth where righteousness will dwell. I don't believe the end-times scenarios that have come and gone throughout history.

I believe in Creation. When there was nothing, from the energy of his Person, God created the unfolding Universe, building into the ongoing creative process all that is needed to accomplish his cosmic purpose. I am an old-earth creationist.

How the Bible Got Started

It was a lazy day in heaven. Archangel Gabriel sat at his desk polishing his horn. Through the open door he saw Archangel Michael shuffling up the road, kicking up gold dust. "Yo, Mike!" Gabriel called.

"Morning, Gabe. Got a minute?"

Michael entered Gabriel's office and pulled up a chair. He spotted the horn. "Got a gig?"

"Not in a long while. Things have been really slow."

"That's why I stopped by," said Gabriel. "Want to come along on an assignment?"

"Sure. What's up?

"The Lord wants me to go down and have a talk with Moses."

"Moses? Last I heard he was camped at Kadesh Barnea. Those pesky Israelites giving him more grief?"

"Oh, no more than usual. It seems Moses will have time on his hands these next years, and the Lord wants him to start the Bible."

"What's a bible?"

"Well, it's a special kind of book telling about God's dealings with mankind and what's to come in the future. He wants Moses to write the first part."

"Hey! God's been talking with Earth people from the get go. Like those great stories about the garden, and the first man and woman hiding in the bushes, the big flood. And the tower! That one was a hoot. Why a book?"

"Gabe, never ask the Lord why. The old stories came before mankind knew how to write. Now that they got it down pat, the Lord wants to give them a permanent record so everyone in all time can get the same message. You know how storytellers can get off track."

"Well, if you want a book, Moses is your man," said Gabriel. "Studied at Alexandria U, you know. What kind of stuff does the Lord want Moses to write?"

"First off, the Lord wants him to pull together the teaching stories he gave way back when stories were the only way to preserve and spread ideas. Every tribe on Earth had stories and storytellers."

"Mostly goofy stories," muttered Gabriel, "like gods squabbling; the world perched on an elephant's shoulders; when the elephant moved—earthquake. Stuff like that"

"Exactly. And did you notice how from tribe to tribe the stories had common themes? How the Earth, sun, moon, and stars got started; why bad things happen; why the gods were mad and how to make them happy. With all those myths and legends floating about, God put his truth in stories ancient people could understand. And he located his stories in Mesopotamia, which would become Abraham's home country. The Lord wants Moses to start off the Bible with those stories."

"Makes sense," said Gabriel, picking up his horn. "I'll take this along. You never know."

"Good idea," said Michael. "Better grab a jacket too. Might be cool down there."

Into All Your World

Jesus issued clear marching orders: Go into the entire world and preach the good news; make disciples--learners.

That's a tall order. The world is 25,000 miles around. Well, try this: Go into all *your* world, a small chunk of the big world. That's the world you are accountable for. Our churches maintain a missionary outreach, and we give, but we can't fulfill Jesus' marching orders with our check-

16

books. Our small world needs the good news as much as any place on earth. Only collectively can Christians go into the entire world.

My childhood world was bound by the cracks in the sidewalk and the muddy alley, clearly defined landmarks. My world grew slowly until it included wherever roads led and airplanes flew. Now my world is a 60-room mansion with 63 bathrooms complete with servants and an elevator. Sixty-four people share my mansion.

I have no car; I walk with a cane; I no longer have a pulpit. Ministry ended? Not by a long shot. I have never been more content or more filled with a sense of mission. I rolled up my missionary sleeves one day and cleaned a kitchen floor, washed dishes, and carried out trash for a neighbor who needed temporary help. My pay: a warm hug. I shared my faith with a broom, dishcloth, and plastic bags.

Two missionaries were talking one day, one from Japan with its millions, the other from rural Alaska with a few hundred. The Japan missionary said, "How could you give your life to so few when over here millions await the Word?" The Alaska missionary replied, "God didn't make me responsible for the people who are not here." He continued, "How many attend your church?" "Ten or twelve. This is a tough field." "Our church is full," said the Alaskan,

At Woodland Garden Apartment I'm one of the guys. No one heeds my ordination certificate. I enjoy our Bible study group led by a warm-hearted Lutheran pastor. I do nothing religious except now and then bless a group meal. But sometime a floor needs cleaning, dishes done, or trash hauled. I suppose I should look for some way to serve Jesus.

The Bible: How did we get it?

That big book on our shelf: We somehow assume it has always been one, unified book. The fact is, nearly 3,000 years passed from the Bible's first manuscript to the first gathering of many separate writings into a single, portable volume. Moses wrote about 1,500 B.C. Gutenberg's Bible appeared in the mid-1400s A.D.

The Bible is an anthology, a compilation of 66 narratives by about 40 people over a span of 1,600 years. Each hand-written narrative was copied again and again on parchment scrolls or fragile papyrus pages. The tangled path from Moses to Johannes Gutenberg led through a maze of editors, copyists, and translators.

Theologians fought fiercely to determine which of hundreds of Hebrew, Aramaic, and Greek writings belonged in the Hebrew and Christian canons. They never reached consensus, hence the Apocrypha.

Theologians continue to squabble over Bible matters: the nature of inspiration, interpretation, and, lately, Bible inerrancy. Nowhere does the Bible claim inerrancy, nor does the reliability of scripture rest on inerrancy. God's evident purpose for the Bible was to tell about a coming Messiah (Christ), who would possess all authority (Matthew 28:18). Jesus did not cede his authority to the Bible or theologians.

Each part of the Bible must be viewed in its historical context and in the context of ancient literature. Inerrancy faces many challenges. Consider one: the exodus.

According to Exodus 12:37-38 and Numbers 1:26, the company Moses led out of Egypt must have numbered about two million. Add them up: 600,000 men over age 20 plus younger men, wives, children, the elderly, and mixed multitude of non-Israelites.

Someone calculated that two million people marching ten abreast would form a line 150 miles long. Add livestock and baggage and you must ask if the arid Sinai Peninsula could sustain that vast company for 40 years. Manna and quail aside, the problems of sanitation, water, supply, communication, logistics, and governance are overwhelming.

I am not suggesting the Bible is unreliable, but we must take into account the nature of ancient literature and the layers of human involvement that followed the original writing. Perhaps some creative scribe got carried away with the exodus drama.

The Ultimate Poverty

I find aging interesting to observe. Over the years I have watched family and friends work through the process. Aunt Esther amazed me. She visited me several times in her 90s, travelling from Oregon alone. She died at 106, still viable.

During pastoring years I devoted much time to nursing homes, serving, learning, and praying I would never wind up there. Then suddenly I found old age approaching. I took inventory.

Though I live alone, I am never lonely. Friends surround me; family live nearby; son Joel invites me to Tucson for winter weeks. A wave of contentment and gratitude overwhelmed me.

I was 90 years old. My apartment holds everything I own. My income is meager but I lack or desire nothing. I move about pain-free, using a cane for balance, and I take one prescribed pill a day. Three score neighbors keep me company and I have a special friend for evening visits. I am as content and fulfilled as ever I have been.

Two questions came to mind: If a million dollars fell in my lap and I could live anywhere I chose, where might that be? What would I buy? I concluded that planet Earth holds no place I would prefer over Woodland Garden Apartments. I might buy another book, maybe two, but I have no needs. As for the million, I would put all of it to work in God's kingdom..

My thoughts went back to a man I encountered in Tucson. He sat alone in the coffee room. I took a chair across from him and wedged into his attention, hoping he would open up.

He warmed slightly but said little. I talked about my life, my faith, and my friends. He looked at me a long moment and said, "I have no friends."

No friends! That must be the ultimate poverty.

The Target

One day Garrison Keillor's *Writer's Almanac* highlighted two of my favorite literary notables: C.S. Lewis and Madeleine L'Engle. I had read Lewis' memoir and two biographies, but I knew little about L'Engle.

I learned in her 30s her writing was going so poorly she considered giving up. Then this sentence in an Albert Einstein book grabbed her: "Anyone who's not lost in rapturous awe at the power and glory of the mind behind the universe is as good as a burnt-out candle."

Fascinated by agnostic Einstein's insight, L'Engle continued reading about theoretical physics and felt compelled to write a sci-fi novel for young people. She titled it, *A Wrinkle in Time.* But 26 publishers rejected the book and she gave up on it.

The *Almanac* reported: "That year, her mother visited for Christmas, and L'Engle hosted a tea party for her mother's old friends. One of those friends was in a writing group with John Farrar of the publishing house Farrar, Strauss, & Giroux....The woman insisted that L'Engle meet Farrar and at least show him the manuscript. He published... *A Wrinkle in Time* (1963). It won the Newbery Medal... (and) sold more than 10 million copies." Madeline died in 2007 as she neared 90.

Her story lends hope as I wrap up my 50-year journeyman literary career. Millions of words, tons of work; how do you measure their worth? Can you imagine agnostic Einstein ever dreamed one sentence from his vast works would jump-start a writing career that would move millions Godward?

I keep thinking: Perhaps someday, some-where, something I write will strike a spark in someone's heart. I turn often to Longfellow's po-em:

I shot an arrow into the air,
It fell to earth, I knew not where;
For, so swiftly it flew, the sight
Could not follow it in its flight.
I breathed a song into the air,
It fell to earth, I knew not where;
For who has sight so keen and strong,
That it can follow the flight of song?
Long, long afterward, in an oak
I found the arrow, still unbroke;
And the song, from beginning to end,
I found again in the heart of a friend.

Like Longfellow's archer I fire away and leave the target to the Lord.

Shed Your Cocoon

Apostle Peter wrapped up his second letter with these words: "But grow in the grace and knowledge of our Lord and Savior Jesus Christ. To him be glory both now and forever. Amen."

As my eighth decade winds down, I hope I have grown in grace and knowledge. Paul nailed it: "When I was a child, I talked like a child, I thought like a child, I reasoned like a child. When I became a man, I put childish ways behind me" (1 Corinthians 13:11.

I'm fond of empty sayings. Here's one: "I'm not the man I used to be, and furthermore, I never was." That's empty only on the surface. At every stage of life, we are split personalities: the persona we project and who we really are. Growing out of that takes time and gumption. Many forces shape how we present ourselves. To grow, we must deal with those forces.

I always believed in Jesus—that was my family heritage. I always believed the Bible, also a family heritage. Scofield's Annotated Bible was the Bible of choice for both my family and church. I bought it lock, stock, and footnotes. Secure in my family cocoon, I was eager to defend the faith once for all delivered to the saints.

Once I considered punching out a boyhood friend who suggested the Bible was a collection of myths and legends. I didn't know what myths and legends were, but they sounded suspicious. He was talking from inside his cocoon.

23

Our cocoon's alpha interpreter shaped my childhood and youth. To grow in grace we must shed the cocoon mentality.

Scripture speaks of kings and thrones, of gates of pearl and streets of gold. Pressing those images into literal molds demeans the truth they are meant to convey. Our faith is laden with mystery. How overpowering to know the God of majesty and mystery invites us into his company.

Best Friend: Someone to Talk to

No matter our age, we never outgrow the need for someone to talk to, someone we can trust with dreams and secrets—a best friend.

When we were kids, we had playmates, maybe lots of them; but there was always a best friend. In time biology kicked in and we sought a boyfriend or girlfriend. Call it puppy love if you will, but puppies grow. Then came mate-seeking. Blessed be the person whose mate is their best friend.

One day we lose our mates, sometimes after decades. Family and friends surround but we grow lonely without a best friend, someone to talk to. That need never leaves.

Have you pondered the chemistry of friendship? Out of many acquaintances we are drawn to a few. Why not all? What turns a good friend into a best friend? We are civil to all, warm toward friends, but a best friend stirs something within.

Best-friendship chemistry is the essence of love. Whatever else we stuff into that abused word, love is the desire to be close, to trust, to share. Youth love is mostly taking; love in mature years is about giving, or it isn't love.

I enjoy conversation with my kids and their mates; I value coffee times with men who share my interests; but for whatever reason, mature years long for companionship with the opposite sex. Such companionship may or may not lead to romance, but inevitably it will grow into affection—a concern to meet one another's needs. Isn't that love's essence?

I am profoundly grateful for the best friend God's grace has supplied; someone to share my memoires, dreams, and secrets. Someone to talk to.

Journey to the Light

Certain of my friends who read this book will shake their heads. Another true believer bit the dust. I would urge them to read my credo and ponder prayerfully the path I have walked for 90 years. I am a devoted follower of Jesus, but I no longer follow some of my early teachers as I search out God's truth.

All truth is God's truth. Theologians have kicked that around at least as far back as Augustine. Any teacher or writer who presents as truth anything that conflicts with what God declares to be true must be wrong. I picked up on that in childhood. What I didn't pick up on was the difference between what God's Word really says and how some of his followers interpret it.

Our church declared with certainty that God created the universe and everything in it in six 24-hour days about 4004 B.C. If scientist claim the universe to be billions of years old, science must be wrong. Our preacher said evil men concocted the theory of evolution to destroy belief in the Scriptures, that Darwin was bent on undermining Christian belief. I recall the scorn heaped on science when what had been presented as the fossilized top of a human skull turned out to be an elephant's knee cap. Obviously, you can't trust science.

My love for nature caused me to waver long before I learned how complex and magnificent God's creation was. I loved rocks and trees, flowers and birds, and stars and pollywogs. The men who shared my love for nature believed in evolution. They became my heroes, but I feared for their souls. They never said one word against God or the Bible; they were churchmen; but they accepted evolution. Carl Rollo, My junior high science teacher believed in evolution. He said not a word against the Bible or chided me for carrying a New Testament, but he didn't think much of Dr. Harry Rimmer, a popular local minister who wrote anti-science books and was a national figure in fundamentalist circles.

The real shocker came in seminary when I learned that Augustus Hopkins Strong, author of our systematic theology text, was a theistic evolutionist. He summed it up: Man came not by

26

the beast but through the beast. Dr. Strong had every smidgen of Baptist theology right except creation. Dr. Adolf Olson explained that Strong, a contemporary of Darwin, was influenced by his times then he moved on quickly. Academic freedom has its limits in a denominational seminary

For me, the clincher came at Bethel Founders' Week when a notable Presbyterian theologian said, "History in Genesis begins with Abraham." That single sentence lifted the shroud.

How Do You Know?

Finding the right title for a book will always challenge writers, but now and then you get lucky. How often does an angry woman standing by the watermelon table at a church picnic hand you both the theme and title for a book you haven't even started? Veteran Hole News readers know the story. You hold in your hands the book.

The angry woman asked me, *How Do You Know that's a Tooth?* The tooth in question is the gnarly black object on the lower right of the cover photo. It is a wooly mammoth tooth dug out of an Alaska gold mine by my friend Roger Green. I told the kids circled for story time that the critter that owned the tooth died about 16,000 years ago.

Declaring that as an unqualified fact is what made the woman angry. She was a confirmed young-earth creationist; I am an unabashed old-earth creationist.

That was not always so, but 50 years of thought, observation, and study changed some of my theological perspectives and deepened my commitment to Jesus. He alone holds authority.

The cover photo symbolizes two sources of truth: the Bible and nature, God's two books. When properly interpreted, they are in full harmony. The Bible reveals Creator Jesus, who brought into being everything there is. God's other book reveals the Creator's majesty and power. Science simply studies what God created.

I believe Jesus is God. I embrace his kingdom, and I embrace science. While some scientists reject all forces but nature, the ranks of scientists include many committed Christians, some at top levels. Check out http://biologos.org.

I cannot prove God to the satisfaction of skeptics; they cannot disprove God to my satisfaction, hence conflict. Sadly, the side that gets loudest and nastiest claims victory. I'll have no part in that. Truth will ultimately triumph. Meanwhile, I'll keep telling my stories.

Happiness
Keith Mattson

Let me tell you what I know about happiness. It is described in Robert Frost's *The Self-Seeker*. The poem runs on for a few pages telling of a bedridden man recovering from severe damage to his legs in a sawmill accident. He's waiting the arrival of a lawyer from the company to sign a compensation agreement for his injuries. A friend comes to talk him out of settling too soon, before he knows if he will ever walk again. "And, what about your flowers?"

The injured man supported himself with his job at the mill, but devoted his life to the wild flowers in the valley where he lived. He annually cataloged them, searched for them, and wasn't content until he had located every species growing there. It was unlikely he would ever pursue his passion again.

When the lawyer arrives the friend expresses his feelings about the impending settlement. The man in the bed tells the lawyer his friend is angry because he thinks the company should pay him for his flowers. But the love of flowers cannot be paid for because it is what he has to give, what he can lavish upon others for no reason but the joy of it. Five hundred dollars will do for his legs, but no money is needed for what he gives away.

Two days ago grandson Ephrem and I went to Nicks Restaurant for breakfast and found one waitress doing the work of three. She was haggard, beset by impatient customers, and only loyalty to her boss kept her from bolting. Eventually we got our food. There were no coffee refills. The bill was $10.63. I decided a ten dollar tip was appropriate and left happier than I'd been in a couple of weeks. If you believe what you have is yours to keep, I doubt you will ever feel you have enough and will seldom be happy.

Oscar Hammerstein put it this way: Love in your heart wasn't put there to stay. Love isn't love till you give it away.

Who Lit the Big Bang?

After a particularly crinkly Hole News post that challenged conventional thinking on Genesis' creation account, a pastor friend emailed: "What is your internal evidence?" Here's how I responded.

You open a can of worms, my friend. The debate has gone on a long time. I can produce no solid evidence for my view, but given the nature of ancient literature, might not Genesis 1-11 be built around God-inspired stories carried by Abram from Ur, the setting for the early Genesis narrative?

Before the advent of narrative writing, oral stories were the only way to preserve and spread ideas. Theologian Merrill Unger claimed God gave Moses the Genesis creation account by direct revelation. I'd like to see his internal evidence.

I know my speculation challenges our traditional doctrine, but maybe it needs challenging. No rain on Earth for 1,500 years? A heavenly canopy holding back the water—was the earth flat? The vast, incredibly complex universe created from scratch in 142 hours about 6,000 years ago? Planet Earth flooded and restarted 4,500 years ago? Almost everyone fine-tunes Bishop Ussher's 4004 B.C. creation date, but tacking on a few thousand years won't cut it.

A literal creation interpretation shoots down every physical science and generally-accepted history. I can't buy that. My inspired-story theory would speak God's truth to people of the time, and largely resolve the Bible/science conflict. I buy Francis Collins' *BioLogos* view. Collins is no Bible-hating liberal.

I put it this way: God, who lives beyond space and time, lit the big bang and continues guiding it toward his planned consummation. I call it *Progressive Creation,* a term I thought original until I found it in Bernard Ramm's *The Christian View of Science and Scripture.*

The Genesis story sets forth a God-directed process: chaos to order, darkness to light, land from the seas, man and animals from dust, woman from man. To many, evolution connotes specie development through unguided natural selection. Had Darwin ever imagined DNA, he would have gone bonkers. Where and how did DNA come from? This is my Father's world, and I think I know how he started it. Whatever the process or time span of creation, God made peo-

ple of such high order that one day he could become one with them.

A Frog by Any Other Name Would Taste As Sweet
Dave Mattson

In her poignant autobiography *Chinese Cin-
derella,* Adeline Yen Mah wrote about a friend's
father who euphemized a menu item in order to
tempt reluctant patrons to try one of his special-
ties. Instead of calling the entrée by its real
name, he listed it as "field chicken." His diners
complimented him on the succulent delicacy,
lightly stir fried and spiced with ginger and soy
sauce. If pressed, he would reveal that the small
drumsticks belonged to a frog.

Which brings us to Luigi Galvani. I don't
know why he was outdoors hanging a copper
wire loaded with frog's legs one day. You'd think
a famous experimenter would have more important things to do. Never the less, while hanging his frog legs, a gust of wind swayed the wire
against the iron railing of his porch. The slight
electric charge the two metals made upon contact set the frog's legs twitching. The rest of the
story, if you do not know it, is worth looking up.
Galvani's contributions to the understanding of
nerves and electricity are honored by devices
and processes named for him.

Poor frog! Whether a misnamed dish or acci-
dental bio-physics experiment, he was given no
choice. From his point of view, losing his legs for
science or culinary was unfair. He, not field

chickens, deserved credit. His sacrifice for science should be named *frogism* not Galvanism.

How many people nursing a miserable grudge feel life is unfair. Their potential thwarted, their just desserts forgotten by an insensitive waiter; they eagerly tell you how cheated they feel. No urging or cajoling will budge them from their cherished wound-licking. They poison all their possibilities with pessimism.

Jonah was such a person. He scowled, "I told you so!" Preaching judgment to Nineveh was a waste of breath. God was all the time ruining a prophet's cherished dream of seeing sinners incinerated. Job's friends were determined to turn his faith sour. How can you continue to trust a God who allows everything to go against you? Even Jesus' family suggested he see a mental health professional.

When your lot in life seems up for sale, let these scriptures reassess your worth: Job 42:1-7, Psalm 11, Luke 2:25-38, Genesis 15:1-7, Numbers 14:1-10, Jonah 4, Luke 16:14-31.

Pastor-Father

She was a friend of a friend, about the age of my youngest son. We have never met. A new Christian, she is untaught in the faith; intelligent, articulate, and recently widowed. She emailed seeking confidential counsel.

Our email exchanges covered wide-ranging issues. One day she wrote, "I was rereading your emails and you never told me exactly what you believed. I would like to hear it. A lot of your emails and your blog are kinda read-between-the-lines. I am daft these days; I need to be told straight out. Can you do that for me?"

How easily we assume we are getting through! We forget how strange the gospel can seem to those without our faith background. I replied:

I wish we could talk face to face. I accept the Apostle's and Nicene creeds—conservative theology going back to the third and fourth centuries. If you're not familiar with them, Google will help.

I believe the Bible, as God gave it, to be his inspired word. I don't believe every interpretation placed on the Bible. For many years I accepted the teachings of my church, never questioning. When I began to probe, some of my beliefs changed, but the Jesus of my childhood faith still lives in my heart.

Jesus founded no church as we know church. Acts 2:42 describes the first Christian gathering: "They devoted themselves to the apostles' teaching and to the fellowship, to the breaking of bread and to prayer." Jesus taught a way of life I seek to follow, that includes a nurturing church fellowship.

My faith accepts mystery, the repository for the inscrutable. My brain cannot fully grasp deity, infinity, eternity, trinity, incarnation—basic Cristian truth. The best anyone can do is speculate on such matters. When we differ, too often we squabble.

Our brain limitation was the reason for the incarnation. We can't know the essence of deity, but we can know a man. So God became a man to teach us all we can know about Him. "No one has ever seen God, but the one and only Son, who is himself God and is in closest relationship with the Father, has made him known" (John 1:18). "I and the Father are one" Jesus said (John 10:30). How can that be? Mystery. Check out Philippians 2:5-11.

We accept Jesus by faith—a kind of knowing. Hebrews 11:1: "Now faith is being sure of what we hope for and certain of what we do not see." I believe in the cross, the empty tomb, Jesus' ascension—more mysteries, more faith.

God gives faith to all who open their hearts to him. Ephesians 2:8-9: "For it is by grace you have been saved, through faith—and this is not from yourselves, it is the gift of God—not by works, so that no one can boast."

As our email exchange continued, my email friend began to call me pastor-father.

The Poison Ivy Caper

I was 13, a First Class Boy Scout with merit badges sewed to my uniform. One merit badge had to do with identifying wild plants, including poison ivy. I knew poison ivy.

One day Father loaded the family in our '28 Chevrolet to visit relatives on a small farm just north of town. When we arrived, our aunt warned us not to go near a bushy vine climbing the fence near the drive. Poison ivy, she explained.

Being a poison ivy expert, I investigated. The vine had the requisite three leaves but it was not poison ivy. To my aunt's horror, I gathered an armful and ripped it from the fence. Rush to the bathroom! Scrub with Fels Naphtha! With all the condescension a First Class Scout can muster, I delivered a lecture on poison ivy.

Someone who presumably knew, someone the family trusted, had declared the vine to be poison ivy. From then on the family lived in fear of a harmless, persistent vine. Had it been poison ivy, I would have known, for I trusted my Scout Handbook and my leaders.

So it is with the church. We all believe what we have been taught by people we trust, assuming they know the truth. Teaching gleaned from elders gets passed on. No one pauses to weigh the teaching, not even when strong evidence suggests it might be wrong. What we really believe is our system. But what if our elders were wrong? That question is not allowed.

It is all right to question the most entrenched belief; even to doubt. Doubting can't harm truth; the Bible will take care of itself. We never own a truth until we test it.

My Box Is Better than Your Box

About one-third the world's population is Christian, one third Muslim, and one-third other faiths or no faith. Scattered across the Christian third are boxes big and small. The boxes are marked by many differences yet they hold three things in common: Jesus, the Bible, and pattern of origin.

Every box or box cluster began with the vision of one person or small group, each claiming to follow Jesus and interpret the Bible aright. The visionary founders built a following loyal to their views. They too often devote more energy defending their views than presenting Jesus to the world. Some boxes will have nothing to do with other boxes.

How curious! From the same Book flow myriads of interpretations. Who can determine which one is right? This is certain: The leaders and dwellers in each box are dead sure they are right.

Boxes go back to the seven churches of Revelation 2. Each was different, yet Jesus claimed them all. That is my point: "We have this treasure in jars of clay to show that this all-surpassing power is from God and not from us" (2 Corinthians 4:7).

Let no one say my box is better than your box. "Who are you to judge someone else's servant? To their own master, servants stand or fall" (Romans 14:4). Jesus loves all his boxes from steepled cathedrals with robed clergy to storefront chapels with cracked windows and Bible-thumpers.

I dwell happily in two boxes: Baptist in the North, Presbyterian in the Southwest. I love them both.

Letter to Grandson Keith

One day grandson Keith, Jr. emailed with questions and comments on his rector's Sunday sermon. Some of his questions involved the mystery of the Jesus' dual nature, God and man. I replied:

The Trinity will always remain mystery, which is why theologians have always struggled with a definition.

My earliest impressions saw the Father as God, Senior; Jesus as God, Junior, and the Holy Spirit as God's rep, the local agent. The New Testament reveals one God functioning as three Persons in relation to his creation, a concept our minds can't wrap around. There can be no hierarchy within the Godhead. I handle it this way: I envision the Father as God transcendent, beyond knowing; the Son as God immanent, revealing what it is possible for man to know about God; The Holy Spirit as God within, nurturing, guiding, applying grace.

Your rector is right on: God is just like Jesus. We must always wrestle with Jesus' dual nature: True God yet True man. Mystery. All visualizing of God is of necessity anthropomorphic, the only basis we have for understanding anything. Jesus was God veiled in human flesh. We catch glimpses of his humanity in Gethsemane and on the cross. More mystery.

Certainly the Bible presents a progressive revelation of God, who always works within the culture of the time while giving glimpses of a better tomorrow. It is folly to try to smooth out rough places in the Old Testament. *The God I Don't Understand* by Christopher Wright discusses four tough questions of the faith. When struggling to reconcile God in history with our culture, faith transcends reason. God needs neither our understanding nor defense.

Knee Jerk

Our book group gathered in the library this afternoon to discuss *The Art of Hearing Heartbeats* by German author Jan-Phillip Sendker, a love story set in old Burma. Jan Krabbe ably led the discussion, a feast for the spirit and mind. Best hour of the month.

My love for Woodland Garden and its people grows week by week. I'm having so much fun, I petitioned Heaven for another ten years. I may have a shot at it: Aunt Esther made it to 106.

A wide-ranging sharing time following the book discussion was equally enriching. Several times I heard, "Lloyd may not agree," referencing my traditional theology. What Lloyd agrees or disagrees with is of no consequence. Karma, clairvoyance, aura, reincarnation, meditation: who am I to gainsay the experience and perception of others? We are all the products of what we have been taught by those we trust, so beware the curse of knee-jerk judgment. Grant others the same respect you hold dear.

"But the Bible clearly says..." If the Bible were so clear, how come so many interpretations? I have rejected several viewpoints I once held sacrosanct. Climbing out of my narrow box was not easy. I dare not lightly dismiss differing views of the Bible and its teachings held by others, and I must attend to thinkers of the past. You can't do theology apart from history, and you can't discuss issues without definitions. Karma by any other name is still karma. Let's have a show of hands: How many know what karma means? You may be surprised when you find out.

Ancient religious and philosophical thinkers around the world embraced truths Christians hold dear because they are true. Truth stands alone, independent of source. The law of gravity is not an option; nor is the power of love, integrity, brotherhood, and justice.

I am a Christian. I believe in Jesus and the Bible. I do not believe every interpretation cast on the Bible. I listen and ponder and *pray*, "Lord, let me not be a knee jerk."

Sneak Attack

The trouble with being a writer is, you're always writing. You write first in your head then on the keyboard. When you are onto something, writing just won't go away.

Over morning coffee one day I was head-writing on how I got to where I was. I recall clearly my childhood church and its theological views, which, of course, I adopted. That's how life works. Over the years I adjusted some of those views, to the dismay of friends.

I doodled to see if I could reduce my present theological posture to a single sentence. Here's what I came up with: I am a Jesus follower, a selective ecumenist, an old-earth creationist, a non-dispensational eschatologist, a sola scriptura-ist (providing I get to define scriptura) and a sanguine saint.

You believe what you will; I'll believe what I will; we'll talk about our viewpoints but we will be friends.

Some rest content all their days in the faith of their tribe. I considered my tribal faith and grew restless. Sometimes change seeps in; sometimes it sneaks up on you. Twice I experienced the sneak attack.

The first attack was seven words from a Presbyterian scholar at Bethel Founders' Week. He said, "History in the Bible begins with Abraham." The second attack was Dr. Clarence Bass's book, *Backgrounds to Dispensationalism.* The sneak attacks challenged my thinking on theology's book-end doctrines: creation and consummation, launching a lifelong study.

With my years winding down, I find myself fully comfortable in my faith and still curious. Mystery heads my credo—things I can't know. I continue to work on what I believe to be true. I lean on Paul's witness in old age: "I know whom I have believed, and am convinced that he is able to guard what I have entrusted to him until that day" (2 Timothy 1:12).

Though a bit winded, I am running victory laps. I value Pastor John Robinson's words to the Mayflower crew and passengers as they were about to leave England: "The Lord hath yet more light and truth to break forth from His Word."

Down with Doomsday

I'm weary of doomsday talk. "Things are so bad, the Lord just has to come soon."

Well, things have always been bad. We just hear bad news faster. Sure, culture change thrusts smut in our face, but porn is as old as cave drawings. Wars and violence are not new.

Have you considered all the good stuff going on? This is still God's world and always will be. He'll close out the present order in his time, exactly according to his plan. I choose to walk in today's light, not stumble through its gloom.

Has mankind ever known a more challenging day? I thought about that as I viewed a video clip, *What a Wonderful World | Playing for Change.* The technology that simultaneously shares the music of kids and musicians from several parts of the world holds great promise.

We are all interconnected. We talk face to face across oceans. Instant notes fly around the globe. World news hits our computers as it unfolds; we're awash with information. What a wonderful world!

To calm your doomsday fears, read *When Time Shall Be No More, Prophecy Belief in Modern American Culture,* Paul S. Boyer. Prophets have sounded end-times warnings since the early Christian centuries.

Calvin and Luther scoffed at Galileo's novel claim that Planet Earth revolves around the sun. How dare an upstart astronomer challenge the Church Fathers? The Bible says Joshua prayed and the sun stood still. If the sun weren't moving, how could it stand still? Know anyone who buys that today? Give that thought the next time someone tells you the Bible declares final judgment is at hand

At, or Over the Edge
Keith Mattson

On hot days children run close to fountains to feel the spray, while grownups hang back in deference to hairdos and clothes, preferring to seek relief in air-conditioned coffee shops. Both kids and grownups get cool, but the kids have more fun, and spend less.

This business of hanging back at the edges of things is good as far as it goes. The view from the Grand Canyon edge is terrific, but nothing compared to a hike or horseback ride down and back up.

According to the Sunday school song, Zacchaeus was a wee little man. He enjoyed considerable social stature as the chief tax collector of the region. Jesus was coming to town. The streets were buzzing. Zacchaeus probably deemed being seen in Jesus' company, at least from the edges, the first-century equivalent to a photo op, but he got there late.

The crowd along Jesus' route was already several people deep. From the sound it, the main attraction was near. Zacchaeus discovered that being at the edge was not close enough, so he did a ridiculous thing for someone of his prominence. Wee little man that he was, like some street urchin, he climbed a tree to see and be seen, and that made all the difference.

You know the rest of the story. If not, check out the 19th chapter of Luke. Zacchaeus got far more than a photo op not by standing at the edge looking in but by stepping over the edge, where life is always more exciting.

The Between

Once there was nothing;
Then there was something.
What came between nothing and something?

God people say God, only God came between.
Everything began with God, whoever God is.
Nature people say Nature, only Nature came between,
Whatever Nature is.
So we're all in the same boat.
Some have God, some have Nature,
But everyone has a Between.

Well, where do we go from there?
What about why, when, and how?

44

When and how go to scientists,
Who know how to figure things out.
Why we give to theologians and philosophers,
Who love to guess about such.

Well, try this:
Once there was nothing; well, almost nothing.
Then there I was, full-blown and breathing.
What came between nothing and me?
Big bang, little bang, whatever;
A tiny wriggler bent on it knew not what,
Against all odds found a friend,
And there you have it: me.

But I did not just pop out
Red-faced, blue-eyed, and bawling.
One cell, two cells, four cells, eight;
A thumb, a brain, an eye.
All I ever would need to be me
Was in that tiny wriggler and his friend.
Isn't that something?

Do you suppose, back when there was nothing,
The Between built into what came after
All it would ever need
To become all it ever would be?
Wouldn't that would be something!

Whistling Ducks
Keith Mattson

It rained much of yesterday in Sarasota and on into the night. I don't know if that was the reason, but the whole flock of fifty some Black-Bellied Whistling Ducks from the lake across the fairway came to the back yard of the condo for only the second time in three years. I watched from my rocking chair on the second floor screen porch as they dabbled in the wet grass until it was dark.

I soon dozed off in the rocker and was immediately beset by bad poets. They came in bunches to me in my sleep insisting I read their poems, all of them short and uniformly awful, the poems I mean. The poets were all rather moody. It was my dream and so I was the expert and they were dunces. They succeeded, however, in reversing the rolls, and accused me of knowing nothing about poetry.

They pushed poems on small slips of white paper in my face. The assignment was to write four lines of iambic pentameter with a simple *abab* rhyme scheme. The poems lacked both meter and rhyme. When I pointed that out they took offense and made me feel terrible for being mean to them.

The bad poets congregated in bunches of eight or ten and sprouted feathers in three shades of brown. High pitched whistling sounds drowned out their grumbling and I awoke in a very bad mood. I looked out through the screen and heard the Whistling Ducks circling, trying to decide if it was still too soon to land. It must have been early because the whistling faded into the distance, so I moved to the bed for a couple hours' better sleep.

A Christmas Prayer

Another year winding down. The Hole News takes up its sixth year, and I find my faith deepened, simplified, and refocused. I count myself a Jesus freak.

In earlier years I filtered my faith through doctrines (Bible interpretations) our gospel clan assumed to be final and irrevocable. Then 50 years of living, observing, and broad reading led me to rethink my clan's views, and I eased out of the box, my faith intact.

Last summer's hospital adventure focused my life on Jesus, the author and finisher of my faith, the one who claimed all authority. Looking death in the eye does change one. I ain't the man I used to be.

I have never lived more confidently or comfortably than now. Psalm 116: 6: "The property lines have fallen beautifully for me; yes, I have a lovely home." (Common English Bible). Unbidden waves of gratitude sweep over me. How can a well-advanced geezer know such joy?

Daughter Sally sent this 15th Century verse. Let it be my Christmas prayer for each Hole News friend:

Lo, in the silent night
A child to God is born
And all is brought again
That ere was lost or lorn.
Could but thy soul, O man
Become a silent night!
God would be born in thee
And set all things aright.

The Crick

The wilderness of my childhood reached from our backyard to the Hill a mile distant. I divided it into zones. My crick flowed through Zone 1. Neighbors called it a creek, but that was not right. Amity Creek, now that was a creek. It flowed comfortably year-around; almost a river. My crick dwindled to a trickle by early summer, though it never dried up. The spring melt or a midsummer gully-buster turned it into a fearsome torrent, and I kept my distance, but when the wild strawberries were ripe, my crick flowed gently.

My favorite spot was a washtub-sized pool alongside a large flat rock which provided an observation point to study pollywogs, mosquito wigglers, and skippers—wiry-legged insects that walked on the water. Jesus bugs. Once I imported minnows from Amity Creek to the pool in a peanut butter jar. They survived for several weeks.

Just upstream from the pool was a red osier dogwood thicket. I cleared space in its center with a hidden entrance for a secret hideout. No one could find me.

Cowslips, bloodroot, and forget-me-nots (Mother's favorite wildflower) bloomed along the crick. An occasional trillium, too rare to pick, grew in the bordering woods. I knew where to find the first mayflowers, bluebells, and violets, blue and yellow. I could name the common birds and trees. I winced on sour pincherries and thimbleberries and puckered up on chokecherries. I feasted on mellow juneberries and found one wild plum tree. Picking wild strawberries and raspberries became annual rituals.

We cut popple (quaking aspen) with abandon to build Robinson Crusoe shelters, but we never cut maple, birch, or oak. Black ash saplings provided crotches for slingshots, which we armed with inner tube strips (red worked best). Soft leather from discarded men's boots made the pockets. We stalked rabbits and partridge and scared a few.

Eggs fried over open fires, overnights in gunnysack tents, bushwhacking to the top of the Hill. I never imagined those boyhood pleasures would one day lead to treks with men and boys on lakes, rivers and mountain trails from Maine to Alaska.

My crick comes to mind when I read Ephesians 2:10: "For we are God's handiwork, created in Christ Jesus to do good works, which God prepared in advance for us to do."

The Memory Channel

When nights grow long and the lonlies come, I switch to the Memory Channel. No commercials, no scenes edited out; I drink from the fountain of youth.

One day I came across field notes from my last Alaska trip:

Alaska! I knew I was back when Lake Clark Air weighed not only my luggage but me. Seven passengers boarded the Piper Navaho Chieftain. A cocker spaniel hopped on and settled in its master's lap as we flew 150 miles from Merrill Field in Anchorage to Port Alsworth, population: 168.

My goal was Tanalian Bible Camp. In 1974 son-in-law Dale Rogers and I joined a work crew to convert an old corrugated-iron airplane repair shop into the camp's first lodge with the chapel on the main floor and kitchen/dining hall in the basement. The lodge served well for many years. I was eager to see the new lodge.

Funded by Franklin Graham's Samaritan's Purse, it was dedicated to Babe and Mary Alsworth, founders of Port Alsworth and donors of the camp property. The new building was striking with a view to die for. Each year hundreds of kids and adults fly in from Southwest Alaska villages for week-long camps and weekend retreats.

Memories welled up. Three junior girls after morning chapel came to talk about Jesus. We went through the scriptures and prayed. The smallest girl with black hair and dancing brown eyes said, "This is the best time I ever got saved!"

Fly fishing for grayling below Tanalian Falls; nighttime coffees with Native men telling stories about missionary Don Stump's early days--their love for Don was palpable. None of them were Christians when Don and Lorene came in 1945 as the lake county's first resident evangelical missionaries. Gillie Jacko's baptism and so much more. Friends and memories—the sum of the good life.

The Memory Channel reminded me of so many good things happening around the World. There's too much gloom and doom. God remains in charge. Noisy politicians and catastrophes come and go, but Jesus never fails.

I'm grateful for a simple faith and my gentle folk religion. If at times I seem irreverent, so be it. Peace and joy, not words, validate my faith. Lord knows I can talk, but an empty heart yields only hollow sounds.

Goodbye Harvey

The trouble with living so long, old friends leave one by one. I thought about that as family and friends gathered to say goodbye to Harvey Sandstrom, 88; my friend for 50 years.

Harvey was competent in all the graphic arts. When I was chosen to lead work among men and boys in our denomination, Harvey designed my logo and brochure. His promo materials helped pull off the biggest men's event in Conference

51

history. A thousand men lined up for a wild game feed at Duluth's Copper Top church.

In 1977 Elsie and I moved to Duluth to serve North Shore Baptist Church. We reconnected with Harvey and his wife Donna Rae. In 1986 they joined the team as we launched the Wordshed Mission. Harvey painted the covers and illustrated our books.

My most rewarding work with Harvey began when I became interim pastor at Fredenberg Chapel, where Harvey was a key leader. Finding the building program in deep trouble, I introduced Harvey to Oden Alreck, a contractor buddy. The project took off. Harvey and Oden became fast friends.

On a slate-colored autumn morning Harvey and I found ourselves cruising toward Isle Royale in Oden's twin-engine fishing boat with four other men planning to troll for lake trout and celebrate Oden's birthday. Half way across, the water pump on one engine failed. We made it to Washington Harbor to spend the night.

The next morning, while Oden and the other men worked on the boat, Harvey led me to the rocky hillside looking westward toward Lake Superior's North Shore. From his shoulder bag Harvey produced a white card and watercolor essentials. I watched fascinated as he painted the scene before us, birthday gift for Oden. I displayed the painting during my tribute at Harvey's memorial service

Harvey honed his remarkable gifts through study and hard work. His art touched people around the world. His paintings hang on Oden's wall and mine, and his friendship will bless our hearts while memory lasts.

Orphan Alice
Keith Mattson

There was a time when kids memorized poems in school. That seldom happens these days. The healing power of the memory bank came into focus one afternoon many years ago.

Alice was the quintessential church lady in a Minnesota congregation I once served as pastor. She was there every Sunday with her children and attended another time or two per week. She served on committees and as a deaconess. After I moved on, she kept in touch with occasional letters and annual Christmas cards.

Twenty years later after I moved, Alice and her husband came all the way to Florida to visit me. She had developed Parkinson's disease leaving her speech hesitant and slurred. She shook noticeably. Her balance was precarious but she didn't like help, so she sometimes fell. She had the bruises to prove it.

Alice lived in an orphanage until she was 18 and went off to college. Years later, on a return to the orphanage for a reunion, she reprised her recitation of James Whitcomb Riley's "Little Orphan Annie," a poem she had recited every year in the orphanage's talent show. I talked her into doing it again in our living room.

After a moment of feigned reluctance, Alice delivered an errorless performance, complete with memorized, deliberately-executed gestures. More remarkable, she recited standing, as steady and erect as a ten-year-old. From the opening "Little Orphan Annie's come to our house to stay" to the final "An' the Gobble-uns 'at gits you ef you don't watch out!" there was no evidence of Parkinson's, not a tremble, stumble, or hint of slurred or hesitant speech. Throughout the recitation Alice was young and whole again.

If you memorized good poems in your early life, I suggest you brush up on them. If no problems live in your memory, there's still time to learn some. You never know when you will need them.

The Last Word
Dave Mattson

The first weapon Japan launched against the United States was a torpedo from a Zero over Pearl Harbor. The torpedo was manufactured by a munitions company in a little-known Japanese town. Smoke and flames covered the harbor as the Pacific Fleet suffered the surprise air raid, and Japanese commanders boasted that once Midway Island was conquered, the United States could be eliminated from the conflict.

Wiser advisors cautioned their leaders not to celebrate prematurely. The battle in the Pacific raged from Alaska to Australia. MacArthur, Nimitz, and Wainwright would become curse words to the Japanese. Ultimately, U.S. forces hounded the Japanese back to their homeland, one island at a time. The last weapon of the war, a bomb dropped over Nagasaki, obliterated the factory where the first torpedo had been made and brought immediate, unconditional surrender.

The Atomic Bomb made a battle to invade mainland Japan unnecessary, sparing hundreds of thousands of American lives and ending Japan's belief in an invincible emperor. The boastful military leaders suffered humiliation for leading the country to ruin.

In Jesus' day, the Romans thought they ruled the world. Religious leaders and kings in Judah imagined they held real power. They crucified Christ and rejoiced, believing that was the final word on Jesus of Nazareth. We can understand their fury when His disciples declared Jesus had returned from the dead.

Every few years some person declares his goal to put an end to belief in God, the Bible, and Jesus. Inevitably, that person is eliminated; most are soon forgotten. God will have the final word, and that word will be Jesus.

Jesus will appear one day as victor in mankind's final battle. We may not live to see that day, but all who have trusted Christ will see Jesus and hear God's final word, Welcome home! "...as many as received him, to them he gave the right to become children of God, even to those who believe in His name" (John 1:12).

Mirage Dads
Keith Mattson

It was Dads' Day at school. Cheryl, normally a tomboyish kindergarten girl, came wearing a frilly dress, anklets trimmed in lace with silk rosebuds, and patent leather shoes. Her dad hadn't arrived when the class left for the program in the gym. She wasn't worried she said, because dad promised this time he'd be here for sure. After songs and poems and skits, dads and kids sat at tables to do a craft project together.

During the program Cheryl's Mom called. Her dad was sick and very sorry he could not come after all. Cheryl suppressed tears when I broke the news. She allowed me to be her substitute dad for the rest of the morning. She made the best of it, but it wasn't the same as having dad there.

Dad's sickness was self-inflicted. He was a heavy drinker and used more hard drugs than anyone knew. He missed Dads' Day because he had been arrested the night before for DUI and couldn't raise bail. Not long after that he died of an overdose.

Cheryl and her mom planted a tree in their yard as a memorial, and in a few days she returned to school with tales of a wonderful dad who brought her presents for Christmas and birthday and sometimes for no reason at all. He worked hard and he got sick a lot and couldn't visit very often, but he was OK now because he had gone to heaven and no one gets sick in heaven.

Five-year-old girls are entitled to good fathers, even if they are mirage oases, loving and inviting from a distance. Just don't try to touch them.

Life's Greatest Achievement
Keith Mattson

Critics tell me I lack ambition. I haven't capitalized on my gifts; made something of myself; achieved something significant. Not true!

Don was a veteran firefighter and I was his hospice chaplain. He was dying from emphysema, the result of breathing smoke and toxic fumes for years before protective equipment for firefighters became standard.

Don was not a good patient. His nurse had to work to maintain compassion. Belligerent and angry, he vented on his caregivers. For some reason, I was an exception. Don was always civil with me. Reports of what a difficult patient he was confused me.

One morning Don's nurse called. Come ASAP. Don was suicidal, asking for assistance to kill himself. When the nurse explained hospice could not do that. Don dismissed her as useless. I found him angry and bored, tired of waiting to die. He wanted it over with. Nothing I said helped.

I hunted out the hospice medical director and reported Don's suicidal feelings. At first she shrugged it off, attributing it to his infamous belligerence. Then she recalled discontinuing his antianxiety medication because he had been in rather good spirits for a week or more. She reinstated the med and he settled into his normal state; crotchety with everybody but me.

I don't know why Don and I hit it off. He warmed sufficiently to me to tell me his life story. He continued to decline and slept much of the time. On one of my final visits, his caregiver welcomed me with a Hello, Reverend. From his bed Don called out, "He's no reverend, he's my friend." He died shortly after.

He's my friend. I banked those words and draw on then when feeling alone. No achievements? I was a dying man's friend. To be a friend or have a friend—same thing—is life's greatest achievement.

Galileo's Telescope

A while back blogger friend Julie Balmer wrote: "Last week I found out that two of the dinosaurs we were so certain of never existed! Triceratops and Brontosaurus. Did you know this?"

No I didn't. I submitted the matter to St. Google, patron saint of everything, and learned paleontologists now believe both critters *did* exist but not as separate species as long assumed. They theorized the boney critters were developmental phases of other species, perhaps something like pollywog to frog.

In my early years I believed pollywogs and frogs were critters unto themselves, of equal value for annoying sister Hazel. I was amazed when higher education (second grade) taught me pollywogs turn into frogs. You sure can't trust a four-year-old.

So should we dismiss science because mistakes crop up? Science is based on mistakes. Every new theory must endure excruciating review as peers labor to disprove it. Scientists love to disprove theories. That's the scientific method. Most scientists welcome new data that shoots down or modifies long-held theories.

In our day, developing tools like the Hubble Space Telescope and more powerful Earth-bound telescopes continually feed in startling new data. The same is happening in very branch of science. Biologists discover new species almost weekly. Paleontologists must revise textbooks continually. God's creation is mysterious, ancient, infinitely complex, and unfolding. Scientific theory will always be changing, but that does not diminish the worth of science. How long did most people, including scientists, believe the sun revolved around Earth? Consider Galileo's woes. Just look into my telescope, he pled.

Leading churchmen would not look. They considered it heresy to even consider the possibility their view of scripture could be faulty, Luther and Calvin among them. They had turf and authority to defend, and the problem continues.

Dinosaurs existed, that is not the question. The question is, when. Galileo's telescope comes to mind. Dare to look. Future generations will thank you.

How About You!

I knew an older man we'll call Frank. Retired from a successful career, he aspired to become a preacher. He was articulate, a heart for God, and a life filled with good experiences. Frank was fun to talk with, but when he got behind a pulpit, his persona changed. He took on a new voice.

That puzzled me until I met his long-time pastor and mentor. Frank was imitating the man's pulpit style down to gestures, pauses, and inflection... Frank's preaching career didn't get very far.

Author/theologian Fredrick Buechner wrote, "Whatever you do with your life—whatever you end up achieving or not achieving—the great gift you have in you to give to the world is the gift of who you alone are; your way of seeing things, and saying things, and feeling about things, that is like nobody else's. If so much as a single one of you were missing, there would be an empty place at the great feast of life that nobody else in all creation but you could fill."

Ephesians 2:10 tells us we are God's handiwork, created in Christ Jesus to do good works, *which God prepared in advance for us to do*. God equips each just right for our life assignment.

My friend Roger often uttered this lament: "I wish I could do something for God." I chided him; he was one of the finest men I ever met. I valued Roger for who he was, not for what he could do. No man enriched my life more. He was my best friend until he died.

A young Chinese woman attended Roger's memorial service. She was into advanced studies for ministry. She had come to Duluth from China as a grad student in a different field. She began attending a Bible study led by a former missionary to Taiwan that met in Roger and his wife Lois' home. Week after week students filled their living room, eager to observe American culture. At one session, the young Chinese woman embraced Christianity.

Roger and Lois' gift of hospitality became part of the endless stream of providence that fulfills God's purpose. Our task is to be what God made us; he'll tend to the doing.

Plant a Garden
Dave Mattson

Times were tough. Jobs were hard to find and paid little. Most folks plodded on, digging into their hearts for grit to make it another day in their tarpaper and tin shanties. Photos from migrant villages of the 30s tell a lot about the kind of people who lived in them.

Then there were those who looked for an easy way out. A flirtatious girl named Bonnie took a job in a cheap roadhouse near Dallas, where she tied in with a drifter who had hacked off a few toes to get out of work while in prison. Bonnie and the drifter joined the Hamilton brothers, robbing banks. In the process they murdered 15 people.

The Hamiltons got caught, but Bonnie and her boyfriend escaped. They hid out, surviving by robbing small stores. Then Bonnie burned her left leg badly during a shootout with sheriff's deputies. She never walked again. In constant pain and hounded by authorities, they sometimes could not stop for food. Once they were reduced to eating a jar of salve. They carried an array of weapons and vowed never to be taken alive.

On May 23, 1934, a posse led by Frank Hamer, one of the last old-time Texas Rangers, ambushed the fugitives on a rural road along the Texas-Louisiana border. Bonnie Parker and Clyde Barrow's easy way out of the depression became a dead end.

But back to the plodders: Depression-era photos show small gardens alongside many shantytown shacks. The plodders responded to hard times with hard work; families did whatever they could to make it. Some went to school so they could succeed when better times returned.

Remember the plodders when life gets tough. Grabbing the easy way out changes nothing. A man with a hoe can feed himself and others; a coward with a gun or a lazy con man can't feed even himself.

When tempted to seek an easy way out, plant a garden of prayer. God will supply the courage to face whatever you fear.

Get Out of the Boat

Matthew 14:23-32 tells the story of that stormy night on Galilee when Jesus walked on water. Being who he was, Jesus could do that. But we forget how much courage it took for Peter to get out of the boat. Sure, he didn't make it all the way, but he went a lot farther than the men who stayed safe. Safe will never change lives.

Peter failed. He got wet. Risk takers often fail. But even as Peter failed his faith grew. He felt Jesus' hand in his. He learned Jesus' willingness to meet human failure. You can't learn that sitting in the boat.

To follow Jesus, we must get out of our comfort zone and go one on one with him. You needn't look far for stormy waters. Men, women, and kids are crying for help. Everywhere, families, communities, and churches are in trouble. We could form a committee to develop a relief strategy; or we could get out of the boat. Jesus never sent a committee to meet a need.

Storms can rage on dry land, too. Remember the traveler who got mugged on the Jericho road? Two leaders of the religious club walked by on the other side, no doubt intent on their agendas. The Samaritan crossed the road. He didn't qualify for the insiders club, but he crossed the road. You know the rest of the story.

Proper religion is fine, but when you've been mugged you need a Samaritan. Dare the unusual, even high-risk stuff. Someone close to you is sailing rough seas; someone got mugged. Get out of the boat; cross the road. Don't worry about failing; Jesus is always close at hand.

The Magic Carpet

The primary meaning of the Bible is what each writing meant to its first readers. Unless you subscribe to the idea that God dictated the Scriptures, you must conclude that ordinary writers using ordinary words following ordinary literary laws gave us the 66 writings that make up the Bible. They wrote over a span of 1,600 years in Hebrew, Aramaic, and Greek.

Moses wrote in the late middle Bronze Age, the period when narrative writing was just developing. Obviously, later editors worked over Moses' text.

I ask repeatedly: How did God speak to mankind before writing was developed? Stories and storytellers were the only possible way to preserve and spread ideas. Hence the legends and myths of all ancient people, and, I am convinced, the stories that make up the first chapters of Genesis. This does not demean Holy Writ. God used what was available.

We take words and writing for granted. Words are not static, colorless building blocks. In *Moon Tiger*, Penelope Lively wrote, "We open our mouths and out flow words whose ancestries we do not even know. We are walking lexicons. In a single sentence of idle chatter we preserve Latin, Anglo-Saxon, Norse: we carry a museum inside our heads, each day we commemorate peoples of whom we have never heard."

Words are magic carpets that carry us to Mars, the stars, the steppes of Asia; to the corner drug store or the lands of Moses and Jesus. Words differ in how they are used. Some have fixed meaning. Others are mobile: pictures, imagery. We recognize literal and figurative speech, prose and poetry. English 101 identified the common figures of speech. A figure of speech is the use of a word or a phrase which transcends its literal interpretation

Non-literal language is essential to the writer's craft, including Bible writers. Sometimes, non-literal language is the best way to communicate literal truth. Think Aesop's Fables and Jesus' parables.

Let us not dumb down God's word.

Put your Fork Down

Today's lecture concerns how to keep growing old. Denial is useless; old will come. But perhaps we can slow it down.

First, we must learn to live with our limitations and look both ways before crossing the street. Your step will slow, your vision cloud; people will begin to mutter. Arthritis will do its thing. You accept that 90 ain't 19. The place to take your stand is your brain. If you are content with TV and naps, you're on the way out.

I live for good books and good conversation. Jog your mind with disciplined reading, and jog with friends; it's more fun. I delight in our Woodland Garden Book Club gatherings.

Conversation must reach beyond pain, pills, and bingo. I enjoy talking with my kids, the Sage of Juniata Street, and my very best friend. We range far into the past and future.

Speed-reading may fit somewhere, but a book you can speed-read is probably best left unread. Like a good meal, you must not gobble a book. Put down your fork now and then. Author André Maurois said, "The reading of a fine book is an uninterrupted dialogue in which the book speaks and our soul replies."

At one time I directed laymen's work for our denomination. One of my goals was to stimulate good reading. One weekend I polled attenders of a large men's retreat to sample reading habits. Of the few who responded, only a handful had read a serious book the previous year. One super-saint said The Bible is all we need.

I have news for him. Unless he is fluent in Greek, Hebrew, and Aramaic, he needs books to wade through the begats.

Some books I choose just for fun. But whether fiction or nonfiction, I search out reading that makes me put my fork down.

The Inerrant Word

Today we explore Bible inerrancy, a hot-button issue. The claim: the original Bible man-uscripts were totally free from error or contradic-tion. A few seem to believe the Bibles on our shelves are also free of from error.

Let's look at one aspect of the exodus men-tioned earlier. Wikipedia: "According to Exodus 12:37-38, the Israelites numbered about six hundred thousand men (age 20 and older) on foot, besides women and children, plus many non-Israelites and livestock. Numbers 1:46 gives a more precise total of 603,550 men aged 20 and up. The 600,000, plus wives, children, the elder-ly, and the mixed multitude of non-Israelites would have numbered some 2 million people. Marching ten abreast, and without accounting for livestock, they would have formed a line 150 miles long."

When Israel marched, the column would stretch from my Duluth apartment to St. Paul's south suburbs with thousands of sheep and goats tagging along. Given the size and nature of the Sinai Peninsula, does that seem feasible?

The children of Israel camped near Kadesh Barnea most of their 40 exodus years. When they marched, the procession strains the imagi-nation. Could two million men, women, children, and their flocks survive a whole generation in the arid Sinai? Manna and quail aside, consider sanitation, water, pasture, and logistics.

I accept the fact of the exodus; I question the reported size of the crowd. It seems evident the author or later editors exaggerated a mite. If that proved to be true, would that nullify the Bible's authority?

We need to look at the nature of ancient literature and God's intent for the Bible. Its authority does not rest on inerrancy. The Bible teaches inerrant truth and God will fulfill his global purpose no matter how we view his book.

I believe God gave the Bible to announce Jesus to the world, the God-man who claimed all authority in heaven and earth. The Bible's message is Jesus, God's inerrant Word. See John 1:1-5 and Hebrews 1:1-3.

Young Earth Old Earth: The Key Issue

The title to this book asks a two-part question, moving from generic to specific. How do I know anything? There are rules for learning/knowing. What happens when something I learn seems not to square with the Bible?

That tooth, for example (see front cover, lower right). What made me think it was 16,000 years old? Since all truth is God's truth, if the universe is only 4,000 or so years old, I must be wrong. But perception and truth are not always the same, a point my poison ivy story makes. An unreliable source misled my horrified aunt. I knew poison ivy from reliable sources: my Scout handbook and a sound teacher.

Is the universe only 4,004 years old? To those who hold to a literal Genesis creation account, it is. But most Bible scholars through history have held the first chapters of Genesis to be figurative. That is the nub of the Bible/Science debate. Until it is resolved, there is nothing to talk about. Neither tradition nor deep conviction determines truth.

Literalists must abandon all the physical sciences or explain discrepancies between a young universe and the findings of science. The 4,004 date was calculated by Bishop Ussher in the 18th century. That would put Noah's flood about 2,300 B.C.E. Those dates generate enormous problems in the light of science. Viewing the Genesis creation and flood accounts as God's teaching stories (figurative) erases the problems.

Here are literalist explanations I have read or heard for apparent discrepancies with science, opinions not necessarily held by all young-earthers:

God created a mature earth just as he created Adam a mature man, giving the appearance of age. God created Earth with light from distant stars already in place. Sciences age-dating systems are unreliable. Scientists make many mistakes, why should we trust them to be accurate on the age of the universe or life development?

Concerning Noah's flood, with six-mile deep water covering the world for a year, they say the mountains were less high then requiring less water. The continents had not separated, allowing all animal and bird species to reach the ark.

The rush of abating flood waters gouged out the canyons of the world. Thousand-mile-an-hour winds blew the tops off mountains burying decaying carcasses accounts for fossils. If there were dinosaurs, they were on the ark.

Though a host of writings exists to explain the literal view, I have not heard or read how flora, pollinators, and other insects survived to re-establish their species, or how a leaf-bearing olive tree survived a year under water.

I believe history in the Bible begins with Abraham. I admire true scientists, God's technicians. I delight in God's teaching stories given to mankind before narrative writing was developed. I love God's two books: the Bible and Nature. I know what I know from them.

What's the Hurry?

In a Fresh Start devotional Jeannine Sawall took readers back to Easter morning. Peter and John had rushed to the open tomb: "(Peter) saw the linen cloths lying there, and the face cloth, which had been on Jesus' head, not lying with the other linen cloths, but folded up in a place by itself" (John 20:7 (ESV)).

Folded up in a place by itself. That grabbed me. Jesus took his time. His earthly mission was finished, certainly an exhilarating moment, yet he paused to fold his facecloth.

I hurry way too much. That's taxing when you're running low on hurry. Through the years I took on too much. Just because you can do something doesn't mean you should. But we must be about God's Work, you say. God's work? Give that some thought. We don't *do* God's work; we are his work.

Nail this to your doorpost: "It is God who works in you to will and to act in order to fulfill his good purpose" (Philippians 2:13). We can work ourselves to death and get nothing done

God's work and church work may not be the same. Churches also get too busy. God's work is a smile, a handshake, a pat on the back. We get tired; and tired people get cranky. Cranky people squabble and grow sour. Who wants to attend a sour church?

Squirrely church kids underfoot? Good. Men's group off fishing for the weekend? Fine. Women away on a quilting retreat? Great. Preacher golfing again? There's hope he will last. Who says we must be tired to be holy?

Too much busy work! Next time someone asks you to serve on a committee, tell them you have a date that night with your spouse; or maybe a bass fishing trip with the kids; or a quiet evening at home with a book.

All the above are God's work. Jesus never assigns a task that will cause you to fail him in another area of life.

Always be about God's work, and that might involve religion. Take your time. Remember the facecloth folded up in a place by itself.

I Can't Live Here Anymore
Dave Mattson

"I can't live here anymore," said the woman. She sat in her dingy kitchen talking to a social worker fresh from college. He studied the chipped paint, drafty windows, and leaking faucets. Her tired eyes, stooped shoulders, and janitor's uniform said it all. The social worker thought he understood.

He arranged for the apartment to be redecorated. He helped the woman find a job handling mail in a nice office. He arranged for new living room furniture. His life goal was to help people in need. Two weeks later, the woman's message on his answer machine shocked him. "I really thank you, but I just can't live here anymore."

Why was she so ungrateful? The social worker stomped to her apartment and again found her in the kitchen. "What's wrong with the new furniture? Why can't you live here anymore?" The woman put both hands over her face and sat a long time.

"I sit in the kitchen because I can't bear to be near the living room window. Seven years ago I leaned out that window to call my daughter home. I could see her just up the street with her friends. I always called her in because rowdies came just after dark. That night they came early. I heard them insult my daughter, and when she fought back, I watched as they killed her and laughed. I just can't live here with those awful pictures haunting my mind."

The social worker stood helpless, ashamed for his anger and false assumptions; for his failure to probe more deeply the woman's need. All he could do was promise her an apartment in another part of town.

To meet the deeper needs of those we would serve, we must take time to listen. Then we can gently teach.

"The Lord is near to those who are discouraged; he saves those who have lost all hope" (Psalm 34:18).

Accredited Prayer

Prayer is talking with God—and listening. The question before us today: Does God hear the prayers of people who do not dwell within our theological boundaries? For example: Could a Kenyan tribal ceremony for comfort and healing help a hurting man? Well, something sure helped—I got well when I was supposed to die. I welcomed all the prayer I could get, whatever its source.

During my heavy-duty illness, bedside prayers included those of a Catholic chaplain—a kind, caring woman; an Episcopal deacon—her concern was evident; my beloved Baptist pastor, assorted family and friends, and a young caregiver from Kenya. I gratefully received her blessing. A drowning man does not ask to review the lifeguard's credentials.

Ham on Nye Missed the Point

Ken Ham (Creation Science president) and Bill Nye (Science Guy (TV entertainer) held a widely-distributed Bible vs. Science debate at the Creation Museum in Kentucky in February, 2014. The debate raised the usual tired issues but danced lightly over the one issue that matters: Is the biblical creation account literal or figurative? Everything in the ongoing debate hangs on that.

The literal viewpoint challenges all the natural sciences plus commonly-accepted history. No amount of speculative reasoning can change that. A universe created from scratch in six 24-hour days about 6,000 years ago can never be reconciled with contemporary science or history.

Viewing the Genesis account as figurative allows Christians to enthusiastically embrace true science as the ongoing exploration of God's universe. I say true science because some scientists, by no means all, deny the existence of a creator.

They share an error with Bible literalists. They assume their viewpoint to be unassailable truth and bludgeon opponents with that assumption. I am an old-earth creationist, one of millions through history and around the world who embrace both the Bible and true science.

As I say often, God lit the big bang and built into it everything necessary to accomplish his purpose. I use the term progressive creation.

You can't do theology apart from history. The work of Bible scholars from other times and places matters. Most theologians past and present positioned themselves on the figurative side, pointing to figures of speech and stories found in all ancient literature. The Bible's 66 separate writings include endless figures of speech. Jesus taught through parables

How did Creator God teach and preserve truth before the advent of narrative writing? Stories were the only means available. Every people group had legends and myths; they honored their storytellers. Is it unreasonable to believe that God taught through stories? Making the literal view of the first chapters of Genesis a test of orthodoxy flies in the face of history.

Science will continue to expand and change—that is the nature of science. But God's truth will remain steadfast, including truths he taught through stories.

Taboo or Not Taboo?

Oliver Wendell Holms, Jr. observed: "We are all tattooed in our cradles with the beliefs of our tribe; the record may seem superficial, but it is indelible. You cannot educate a man wholly out of superstitious fears which were implanted in his imagination, no matter how utterly his reason may reject them."

One afternoon in early youth I came upon a dime and opportunity to attend a movie unobserved. I don't recall the title—that didn't matter.

By long Baptist tradition, movies were taboo, along with dancing, drinking, smoking, and playing cards. I sat through the show nibbled by fear. What if the rapture occurred (always imminent) and the Lord found me in a theater? I might get left behind, a veiled threat. The threat applied to all our taboos.

Even as a kid I saw inconsistencies. Our church approved of roller skating parties in the same venue as dances with the same music. As I recall, we held the girls as close as possible.

Regular playing cards were forbidden, but Rook cards were OK. Colors replaced symbols for suits; all else was the same, including games. We were told regular cards represented gambling, yet dice were OK. We threw dice to chase one another around the Parcheesi board. At a casino (also taboo) and on the street, dice had considerable to do with gambling.

Alcohol in any form was also taboo, Jesus' wedding party notwithstanding. He turned the water into unfermented grape juice, evangelists told us, for God wouldn't make something harmful.

I recall discomfort one evening as Elsie and I met in a restaurant/lounge with the board of a newly re-organized Christian camp. The leader and benefactor, a non-Baptist, emerged from the bar with a drink, which he fingered as he laid out his vision: We will do our best to provide a setting where God can touch the hearts of kids, but we must always rely on the Holy Spirit. The following years demonstrated his spiritual commitment to the camp.

Can God bless a ministry led by a man who drinks? I heard someone mutter, God would bless more if he didn't. What was it Oliver Wendell Holms, Jr. said about superstition?

Assignment: Miracle
Keith Mattson

It was one of those days. On an impulse I drove into the parking lot of the branch library with nothing particular in mind but a vague need to lay my hands on something new to read or music to add to my collection.

A few minutes among the several thousand CD's convinced me music wasn't what I wanted. I turned to the library's first calling: books. Libraries are wonderful places to wander. Aisles of knowledge: biography, history, politics, theology. Newly-released books of all genres.

I found three meager shelves devoted to poetry, mostly collected works of a single poet or anthologies of a particular time span or nation. Among the one-poet books I found three small volumes by Mary Oliver I did not have in my collection.

Three days passed. Finally, in my recliner by the study window, I took up the books. I disciplined myself to read one from first poem to last, pausing occasionally for reflection. That done, I turned to the next title, which included essays as well as poems. This time my discipline failed. Three lines stopped me:

So quickly, without a moment's warning/ Does the miraculous swerve and point to us,/ Demanding that we be its willing servant.

Typical Mary Oliver; the simplest of discoveries prompted that assertion. She was cleaning a fresh-caught bluefish on the ocean shore near her home. She found the fish's stomach full of just-eaten sand eels, some still wriggling. She released the little eels back into the Atlantic, restoring lives they had lost.

The lines triggered memory of a night the miraculous swerved and pointed to me. A little east of Cincinnati, a battered car westbound on I-71 carrying a scraggly young couple stopped at a gas station, almost out of gas. I pulled in shortly after to top off my tank and hopefully find a sandwich.

I noted the couple had only a handful of change dug from the woman's purse and nooks and crannies in their car. They were headed for Louisville, Kentucky. I had lots of gas and travel funds. I bought them a tank of gas. I had no choice. They bought a cup of coffee and were taking turns sipping as I drove away.

Another item on my list of worthiness claims. I was once a dying man's friend, and that night I was a young couple's miracle.

Me and My Harmonica

A while back an Alaska friend sent a link featuring Buddy Green's incredible harmonica performance in Carnegie Hall. I know the harmonica well; been playing since age six. Where Buddy finds what he does in a twelve-hole harp blows my mind. He exemplifies the adage: Talent is a license for hard work.

Blessed with musical genes, I played many instruments over the years, but I mastered none. I honor artists, artisans, and scholars in any field, including religion. But what does God think of their achievement? We tend to limit pleasing God to things religious, as though spiritual values end at the church door.

That's the dreadful dichotomy I write about often. According to scripture, every moment of life is sacred and holds equal spiritual potential. I love my church, my Bible, and prayer times. I regularly ponder things eternal. But worship and devotions consume but a small fraction of the day's hours. What about the rest of the day? Check out Philippians 4:8: "...whatever is true, whatever is noble, whatever is right, whatever is pure, whatever is lovely, whatever is admirable— if anything is excellent or praiseworthy—think about such things."

Paul presents life qualities that cover the waterfront of wholesome living. There's not a devotional exercise among them. Must a story, song, painting, sculpture, or poem follow a religious theme to please God? Apostle Paul didn't think so.

In my early youth Uncle Hans gave me a battered trombone. I taught myself to play fairly well. I aspired to play in the high school band but I needed a better instrument. When I hinted at a new horn my father said, "What good is a trombone?"

He associated horns with dance bands. I guess he feared I would be led into sin. I thought to remind him that famed gospel singer Homer Rodeheaver played trombone, but I let it go.

I did get fairly accomplished on the harmonica, but neither Nashville nor Carnegie Hall has called.

Sacred Cows

My Hole News post one day included back-cover copy for this book which spoke of herding sacred cows. What sacred cows?

To start with, the Big Five of my childhood and youth: dancing, drinking, smoking, card playing, and movies; all taboos that became sacred cows. Some churches added shooting pool. A pastor friend came to a new congregation with a Carom board and cue sticks. Finger-flicking caroms would be OK, but cue sticks smacks of pool. The pastor tucked the board behind the piano and left it there until he moved.

Ridiculous! Well, how about the taboo police of my youth who eagerly sought out movies on early TV, movies they forbade me to watch in a theater?

Hindus hold some cows sacred, but not work cows—oxen. That pick-and-choose. That attitude spilled over on Christians. My old-earth creation view banned me from a pulpit. I shudder to think what might have happened had they known I almost baptized a baby. Tar and feathers? Burning at the stake was banned a while back.

What is more important: a dear Lutheran grandmother's peace of mind or a scruple? I'll go with Grandmother. I know all about *baptidzo.*

I shocked a long-time friend by questioning Dispensationalism. "You don't believe in the rapture?" I explained I believed that 1 Thessalonians 4:13-18 and 1 Corinthians 15:50-52 would surely take place, but not on John Darby's schedule. My friend had never heard of Darby, the Brit who created Dispensationalism in the mid-1800s. Venerable Baptist Spurgeon thought that teaching strange.

I don't believe the Bible holds a code for determining future dates. Think Harold Camping and hundreds like him. We have made the Bible something God never intended. Few rank and file Christians have any idea of the cultural setting in which the 66 writings appeared or how the Bible came to us. We turn our particular view of scripture into a sacred cow.

What do I believe? I believe Jesus was God become man to teach us all we can know about God. I believe Jesus' atoning death saves us from sin's consequences not only in eternity but now. I wish all who claim to follow Jesus would relate to people like he did.

The only time Jesus spoke harshly was in the company of religious leaders. How gentle he is with sinners like me! Gentle: that's how I want to live.

Buried Treasure

The vicissitudes of aging call for stern measures. Painful though it be, long-held treasures must go, starting with books. Hoarded books, like hoarded dollars, serve no good purpose. I will give appropriate titles to the Woodland Garden library to make space for new titles that continue to accumulate. I can't imagine life without books.

Next I'll purge old files, some reaching back 65 years. I worked so hard on Greek Exegesis in seminary I could not bear to part with the notes. I have not looked on the pages since. Musty correspondence, old book contracts, yellowing newspaper clips, endless sermon notes, and ragged tear sheets: detritus of the tides of time. Why do we keep ancient bank statements, tax records, and manuals for dead gadgets?

Photos cling the hardest. I'll build a file for family; another for the recycle bin. And 35mm slides! Two bits each. Lots of money in that box. I'll digitalize a few.

Buried treasure stirs sleeping memories. Dead friends come to life. I hike mountain trails and paddle canoe waters again. I smell wood smoke and hear the cry of night birds. I feel the warmth of my lover's embrace, the joys of family. Maybe that's why I saved the treasures, to remind me of a life rich beyond measure.

Lord, let time take mobility, hearing, even sight; but please, Lord, leave me my memories.

Her Pièce de Résistance
David Mattson

Her husband worked for the government. It was war time. Everyone wanted to do their part to end the fighting with Japan and Germany. She and her co-workers joined the OSS (later the CIA). They were assigned to projects related to covert operatives. Her most notable achievement was a shark repelling formula that protected Frogmen and advance teams directing amphibious landings. Like thousands of other anonymous patriots, she considered her achievement a small part of the war effort.

You may know some of this woman's other recipes. Julia Child brought a love of fine cooking to the world as one of the first televised super chefs. Her signature rich voice and equally rich entrees paved the way for networks of cooking celebrities. It is difficult to picture Julia, the consummate gourmet, as a lab-coated scientist.

It was equally difficult for people to picture Jesus, that carpenter of suspicious parentage, as the Messiah. Even more difficult to believe his rude collection of followers could be prophets of the kingdom of heaven. Neither Jesus' message nor his messengers were what people expected. It was as though the God of heaven had deliberately chosen Earth's least impressive channels to reveal himself to mankind.

God did not stand on his head, produce a savory recipe you're willing to swallow, or hire a celebrity to lure you to give him a chance. That's not God's way. Jesus had all day for a woman who was currently shacked up with her sixth loser. He picked a petty, thieving, tax collecting bureaucrat to visit for dinner. Little children, desperate beggars, and bawdy fishermen were Jesus' style. There's something about people who cannot pretend to be other than they are that draws divine revelation.

Pride is a sickness that robs people of integrity, holding them prisoner to deceptive fears. Faith will humble you, but not humiliate you. The philosopher always runs out of time before questions. You can be one of the wiser, nobler types who, as Jesus approaches, look the other way. Or you can say with hymn-writer Fanny Crosby, Savior, do not pass me by.

What's Your IQ?

Recently someone asked me about my IQ; I don't recall why. I have no idea the number, nor am I overly curious. No one ever labelled me brilliant or particularly dull. I drifted midstream through life, managing to get by, often surprised where life took me.

Childhood reading gave me a respectable vocabulary, cultivated my imagination, and sired the idea that maybe I too could write a book, an idea I hid—I was nine. Thirty years later my first book appeared. After 52 years of writing, editing, and publishing, you hold what is likely my final print book. E-books remain an option.

You will find the next pages a hodgepodge, little more than stream-of-consciousness narrative. "Stream of consciousness is a narrative device used in literature to depict the multitudinous thoughts and feelings which pass through the mind. Another phrase for it is 'interior monologue.'". *A Dictionary of Literary Terms,* J. A. Cuddon.

My life was a stream of consciousness; like stories I wrote, seldom planned. I never knew when I began a story where it would go. That was the fun of writing and, in retrospect, the fun of living. I learned to pack light for I may move in the morning.

Many entries on these pages first appeared in the Hole News, now in its sixth year. A stream of consciousness if ever there was one. The Hole News began as a group email to my family and close friends as Elsie entered the valley. I expected the emails would cease when Elsie died, but, unaccountably, the list grew and continues to grow. My ramblings seem to meet a need.

The value of a book or blog lies not so much in what it says but in what it causes the reader or to think. Thus it is with these pages, and with my life.

My Friend the Atheist

"It's my God-given right to be an atheist!"

I doubt anyone ever said that, but it speaks a truth. The God idea seems intuitive; every culture through history has exhibited a sense of the supernatural, a force behind nature and history. It takes considerable effort to free the mind from the God idea. To view the universe apart from an external cause takes a leap of faith.

Christians shouldn't be too hard on atheists, for they also seek truth. What Christian has never wondered deep in his heart, where did God come from? Like atheists, Christians need a faith leap to accept God's existence.

The Bible assumes God; it makes no attempt to prove him. God is not the subject to proof. We can offer many supportive considerations, but not empirical evidence.

I believe in God (belief and faith, same word in the Bible), but where did my belief come from? I did not sit down one day, lay out options, and go with God. My parents, relatives, and close friends were Christians. Had they been Jewish, Muslim, or Buddhist, I no doubt would have followed their belief.

Be humble in our faith claim for faith is a gift from God. Jesus said, "You did not choose me, but I chose you..." (John 15:16). If you possess faith, never cease to be grateful. Walk respectfully among those who lack faith.

We cannot weigh or measure faith or package it as a commodity. Our best faith definitions and analogies fall short. We can only demonstrate faith by what it produces in our life. How we live is our only argument to draw others to faith.

What about the Bible? The Bible has no authority for those who don't believe it. The Bible's power lies in its story—the Incarnation. Only Jesus can draw people to himself. We are only agents, salespersons. Our life is our sales pitch.

Mystery

I love my Woodland Garden home with its unspoiled view of God's other book. One morning a resident photographed a bobcat scoping our pond. The cat must have been hungry to show itself in daylight. Deer walk through daily. One night coyotes yipped close by. Canada geese are regulars; a bald eagle flaps by now and then. Legend has it a wolf once came snooping.

Critters: pictures from God's other book, a handful of the millions of flora and fauna science has classified. Within these species dwell a host of variations just waiting for clever people to release them.

Duluth's rose garden overlooking the big lake displays dozens of varied blooms, all drawn from God's generic rose. The tethered pint-sized fuzzy mops my neighbors pamper all came from basic dog: the wolf. God planted the potential for endless change in his creation and gave mankind skills to produce it. Scientists are God's little helpers.

Sure, some scientists deny a supreme being; they struggle mightily to explain him away. Nature is all there is, they say, but the smartest atheist cannot explain how Nature unaided could produce such staggering complexity, though they try.

By the same token, we cannot muster empirical evidence to prove God. Even our believing minds cannot fully encompass his Being. The best anyone can do is observe and measure God's deeds, which is what scientists do.

God's Person and power must always dwell in mystery. "No one has ever seen God" (John 1:18).

In one corner of mystery I keep a dustbin where I sweep theological conundrums. Let those who will bicker over eternal security, foreknowledge, the Trinity, etc. I am content to leave such matters to God and rely utterly on his sovereign grace.

Then there is Incarnation. I believe Jesus was who he claimed to be, one with the Father. Jesus the God man created and sustains the universe—and me. That's the greatest mystery, and that's all I need to know.

My Kind of Religion

Nature, God's other book, gives us many examples of *symbiosis,* the interdependence of two different species. Certain flowers can be pollinated by only one insect species; and nectar from that flower supplies the insect's only food.

The more I learn about God's web of life, the greater my wonder.

Creator God was profligate with the biosphere; he made millions of species, from amoeba to zebras with behemoths tossed in, all ultimately interdependent. Ever wish God had struck mosquitoes from his list? Don't tell that to some birds; their only food is mosquitoes.

We mortals stand atop the food chain endowed by God with capabilities beyond all other creatures, and he charged us to tend his handiwork. We blew that assignment badly, just as we keep blowing God's plan for our lives. What does Jesus expect of us?

One day a job assignment took me from Chicago to somewhere with a plane change in Seattle. I had just enough time between flights for coffee. As I made my way toward the coffee shop, I came upon an older woman in a shabby tweed coat carrying two loaded shopping bags. She looked this way and that, obviously distressed. The poor woman is lost, I said to myself, and hurried on.

A punch in the gut stopped me. My urgency was a cup of coffee. I turned around, took the woman's bags, learned her need, and walked her to an Alaska Airline gate. I long ago forgot my mission for that trip, but I will never forget the woman's God bless you.

Do you suppose God flew me all the way to Seattle just to answer an old woman's prayer? Why not? He arranged for mosquitoes to feed certain birds.

"Religion that God our Father accepts as pure and faultless is this: to look after orphans and widows in their distress and to keep oneself from being polluted by the world" (James 1:27).

That's my kind of religion.

In the Beginning God

Because the issue looms large on our theological horizon, the Bible/Science debate makes its way several times in these pages. The age of the universe and Darwinian evolution are primary issues.

The debate has no point until we resolve the foundational issue: Did God give the first chapters of Genesis as literal history or teaching stories? If literal, all physical sciences and commonly accepted history are dead wrong.

I live on the figurative side. I believe God lit the big bang and built into what followed all that was needed to produce everything he desired for Earth, space, and mankind. Science explores the *what* and *when* of creation. Theology explores the *Who* of creation. Neither science nor theology can explain creation's *how* or *why*, truths shrouded in mystery.

The Life Application Study Bible (NIV) says this on creation issues: "The Bible does not discuss the subject of evolution. Rather, its worldview assumes God created the world. The biblical view of creation is not in conflict with science; rather, it is in conflict with any worldview that starts without a creator.

"Equally sincere and committed Christians have struggled with the subject of beginnings and have come to different conclusions. This, of course, is to be expected because the evidence is very old and, due to the ravages of the ages, quite fragmented. ...Students of the bible must be careful not to make the Bible say what it doesn't say, and students of science must not make science say what it doesn't say. The most important aspect of the continuing discussion is not the process of creation, but the origin of creation. The world is not the product of blind chance and probability; God created it."

J. Sidlow Baxter, writing in *Explore the Book, Vol., 1* adds this: "In Genesis we have a synopsis of all former revelation, sufficient to constitute a working introduction to the further revelation of God communicated to us in the Bible."

Whenever and however the universe began, and by what processes, most assuredly it is God's handiwork. God built into his handiwork the ultimate consummation of the universe, with a new heaven and new earth to come. It will be surpassingly interesting to see how that works out.

Joshua' Fit de Battle of Jericho
Dave Mattson

Had Stonewall Jackson not fallen to friendly fire, the War Between the States might have ended to the South's advantage. He was able to inspire his men and improvise tactically on the battlefield. Jackson probably was one of the few military leaders who saw that the senseless slaughter of traditional formation warfare was obsolete. It would be after the First World War before men like McArthur and Patton would be given freedom to modernize tactics to fit the weapons of mechanized combat.

Students of warfare realize that victory often depends on more than statistics. Superior numbers of men and bigger bombs can't assure conquest. Victory may depend upon a leader who can devise a strategy that fits the enemy, terrain, and available firepower. Being a general is not enough; the commander must fight the battle at hand.

God commanded Moses to prepare Joshua for future command, making him fit for leading the conquest of the Promised Land. When Israel crossed Jordan and approached Jericho, Joshua was the right man to lead the unconventional warfare that brought the walls tumbling down.

God prepared many men and women in the Scriptures for the special circumstances of the conflict. Gideon's guerilla band caused the enemy to stampede in panic. Esther's courageous stand before the king saved her people and condemned her enemy. Like other biblical heroes, Esther was made for "such a time as this."

God's Word promises to equip each of us for our unique battles. Proverbs tells we have needs only God can help us with. It is easy to let criticism cause us to doubt our ability to make it on your own. Crushing depression, bullying enemies and manipulative seducers can leave us wondering if we are up to life's challenges.

When searching his heart in dark hours of need, King David found a good shepherd to restore his soul. New Testament apostles found a friend who could strengthen them to do all things. And God will help you shoulder your weapon and take the fight to your enemy with tactics that will win.

Read God's Word thoughtfully, pray about what troubles you and fellowship with other soldiers of the cross. You'll make it!

The Gift of Intimacy

Our sex-mad society has all but ruined the concept of love and intimacy. Intimacy is far more than body parts. Intimacy is a soul-to-soul embrace that relishes the company of another person, man or woman. Intimacy happily absorbs differences, listens, learns, and gives.

Yesterday I spent two hours with the Sage of Juniata Street nursing a Mountain Dew at Dunn Bros. Clyde and I haven't philosophized in three months. We worked over world affairs, books, trivia, and personal matters, warmed by the ambiance of a well-filled coffee house.

Laptops flared. An older couple at the table next to ours played cribbage. No distracting music; just the quiet murmur of souls enjoying each other's company.

Clyde and I entered our small world, knit together by friendship, trust, common interests, and mutual respect. Clyde is moving toward 80, a mark I passed a while back. His faith journey differs from mine in some respects, but we arrived at same destination.

He maintains a unique mentoring ministry among young people he meets at Dunn Bros and elsewhere.   I have a roving ministry, befriending strangers who cross my path and pounding my bully pulpit, the word processor.

I often ponder the mysteries of love and intimacy, the closeness of spirit with another that seems just to happen. As years accumulate, you covet the gift of closeness that binds your spirit to another, a closeness that defies definition.

That gift was the heart during my recent overnight in ICU. I walked through Psalm 23 and my cup overflowed.

Have I become a sentimental old fool? Sentimental? Yes. Old? Indeed. If that makes me a fool, I'll take it. How long since you cried over six verses of scripture?

Worn Smooth
Keith Mattson

I'm about half the way through a visit with my father. Every visit now is increasingly precious. He's 88, vigorous compared to most his age, and as sharp of mind and spirit as few ever are. He navigates the steps up and down from his quarters slower and with greater care than my last visit. Next week he will have a colonoscopy to check some irksome symptoms. That gives me pause to reflect on what both of us know: He hasn't nearly so far to go as he has come.

There's nothing maudlin in this. Over the last few years we have grown closer than ever. We've left nothing unspoken that needs to be said. He is still the rock that anchors the family. I think each of my four siblings would say the same.

Dad isn't basking in the richness of life past, he's as engaged as ever. Right now he's in his quarters organizing questions he has for his blind webmaster. Today he is seeking help to upload his 250 name emailing list for the blog he's been writing for the past four years.

Then we will pick up Dad's high school sweetheart Barb at the nursing home where she lives. We'll take her to lunch then on a scenic drive to see the fall color—it's a glorious sunny day. He visits Barb often, takes her to lunch occasionally, and makes her lonely life happier.

Like rocks in a riverbed, time hasn't beaten Dad down. He's been worn smooth by the endless washing of time and circumstance, work and play, friends and enemies, good times and not so good. He fits easily into the life that continues to wash over him with a few sharp edges making just enough ripples to be lovely.

Wrongly Dividing the Word

From the earliest Christian centuries recurring waves of end-times fervor have washed over parts of the world. Earnest Bible students fixed the day when Jesus would return, probing Old Testament passages they believed held the code for unfolding world history. Harold Camping, America's most recent date-setter, had to eat crow, like all who came before him.

American Harold Miller was the prophecy buff in the early 1,800s. His writings stirred excitement in places around the English-speaking world. Miller set time brackets rather than a specific date, but one of his followers set a date, leading to yet another great disappointment.

Miller's speculations fired the imagination of John Nelson Darby, Bible scholar and prominent leader of the Plymouth Brethren movement in Bristol, England, He devised something totally new he named Dispensationalism. Second Timothy 2:1 became his slogan: "Rightly dividing the word of truth."

Darby, along with C.I Scofield in the U.S. divided Bible history into seven segments, the seventh being the millennium. He came up with a concept unheard of among Bible scholars: the secret catching away of believers prior to the great tribulation. He called it the Rapture. One would think such a dramatic event would have caught the attention of at least one theologian, but no trace can be found.

D.L. Moody and other prominent American evangelists picked up on Dispensationalism and made it core teaching in preaching campaigns and Bible schools they founded.

Dispensationalism's greatest boost came through the Scofield Bible, edited and annotated by Cyrus I Scofield in 1909, revised in 1917. It became the most popular Bible version for Fundamentalist/Evangelical America, including my boyhood church.

Bible scholars through history have held a different view of the End Times. The New International Version presents 2 Timothy 2:1 this way: "Do your best to present yourself to God as one approved, a worker who does not need to be ashamed and who *correctly handles* the word of truth." The passage says nothing about *dividing.* It's hard to believe a Greek scholar of Darby's stature overlooked the word's etymology.

Sweetly on the Ear

Nostalgia! Friend Greg Overfors sent me a YouTube link to Sweden's answer to Bill Gaither's band; same instrumentation, rhythms, and harmonies. Only the language was different. I listened for two hours and shed occasional tears.

Part of my childhood was steeped in a gentle Swedish brogue. My scant grasp of Swedish faded long ago, but the tunes and the spirit of the vocalists singing their love for Jesus rested sweetly on my ear. We need to listen to each other; to bond in spirit even when our forms of communication differ.

I love Sunday mornings at Emmanuel. Our worship differs little from services I led 70 years ago. We sing from hymnbooks accompanied by organ and piano. No band, no handwriting on the wall. Mostly grey-tinged worshippers sing their hearts out. Pastor Dave wears a suit and tie and stands behind the pulpit.

A half-mile north and south multi-generation saints from our tribe worship differently, with considerably more noise. But their worship of Jesus rests sweetly on the heart. When families with kids come to our church, we point them north or south. We have no kids' programs save children's church.

What future can a church possess that caters mostly to the community's silver sliver? I won't guess long range, but right now we're trying to figure out how to squeeze in more seating. New folks keep coming.

Ripeness and Rot
Keith Mattson

The ripeness/ of the apple/ is its downfall, wrote Mary Oliver. What brought this to mind was an article about the precarious state of Walmart, the world's largest retailer. According to the writer it is falling apart as we watch. It reads like similar articles about other giant retailers thought invincible but now are gone or in trouble.

There are plenty of reasons for Walmart to fail. Blame the rise of online shopping and cyber giants like Amazon.com; bad customer service; inadequate pay for their employees; or the Great Recession we still haven't recovered from. Maybe it is retribution for all the smaller businesses it supplanted.

Those are all factors in the decline, but none is the cause. The culprit is identified in Mary Oliver's description of the apple. Any enterprise whose success requires endless growth has lost touch with the reality. The time from blossom to the peak of ripeness is relatively long. But the time from ripe to rotten is short.

Churches are not much different. Most are small and hang on from year to year in greater or less prosperity, scarcely more than blossoms and a long way from ripe, but they linger. Some, however, follow an ambitious leader who takes them to impressive size and influence, only to fail altogether or fall to little more than ruins when the leader steps aside. The Crystal Cathedral comes to mind.

So many others have failed. No matter a leader's doctrinal stance, they are susceptible to over-ripeness and eventual rot. Better to follow Jesus into service than track pastors into big auditoriums.

All Has Been Heard

"Now all has been heard; here is the conclusion of the matter: Fear God and keep his commandments, for this is the duty of all mankind" (Ecclesiastes 12:13).

Thus the writer of Ecclesiastes concludes his ruminations on mankind and I can think of no better way to conclude Part One. God is mystery--hold him in deepest awe. He set forth his commandment: Love God with all your heart, mind, and soul; love your neighbor as yourself. That's it. Be at ease; God won't forget any good thing you do. He keeps clean books.

I liken our fuss about serving God to a man paddling a canoe in a cruise ship swimming pool. He rams his craft into the forward wall and paddles like mad, thinking he is moving the ship. We're all along for the ride. We can't serve God; we can only be his servants, filling different roles at his bidding.

Live in Philippians 2:12-13: "Continue to work out your salvation (put it to work) with fear and trembling, for it is God who works in you to will and to act according to his good purpose."

Live in peace. Live quietly. God's love never needs to shout.

Part Two

Originally, Part One ended the book. Then a special friend read some of my past writings and Bob Kelly's collection of quotes and said, "Lloyd, you have to include them in the book."

She was so taken with Paul and Nattie Boskoffsky, she insisted I include parts of their story. I did so in the Epilogue. I'm grateful for her insights. The additions made for a better book.

A Kid's-eye View of the Bible reconstructs childhood thoughts about Bible stories I heard in Sunday school and from the pulpit. Seed thoughts from my early years matured into faith-changing blooms. We must not assume young listeners perceive the Bible the way adults do.

Story Tree tales were created for morning worship kids' times. For youngsters, the lesson is as much the storyteller as the story. You can never win kids' minds until you win their hearts. If the stories bend the letter of scripture, so be it. Sermons often do that too.

The Song of a Man and a Land evolved from a Lincoln's birthday television special built around some remarkably talented teens in Alaska. Whatever you think of the poetry, the message is vital to the future of our land.

A Kid's-Eye View of the Bible

The Bible has been part of my life from earliest memory. Our family read the Scofield's King James Version, which we held to be absolute truth.

The imminent rapture provided powerful incentive for holy living. You wouldn't want to get caught at a dance or movie theater when the Lord returned. I risked a movie now and then but never a dance.

For sure, God created everything there is in six ordinary days around 4004 B.C. That date was printed in my Bible. He started creating Sunday morning, worked hard all week, and Saturday off to rest up, just like my dad, only he rested on Sunday.

God started people with Adam, who he made out of dust. I couldn't figure out how God did that, dust being so dry. But God can do anything. He put Adam in charge of animals, birds, and fish and gave him the job of naming the animals, which was really hard, there being so many.

Adam did as God told him and he kept looking but he found no helpmeet, whatever that was. I figured it must be a wife because one day when Adam was taking a nap, God cut out one of his ribs and carved Eve. I knew about carving. My dad carved neat things from walnut shells, but they were really small. God made Eve almost as big as Adam out of one rib. That's how girls got started.

Then God put Adam and Eve in the Garden of Eden and told them not to touch a certain tree or bad things would happen. The Bible didn't say what kind of tree it was, but apple makes sense. We had crabapple trees in our yard that were pleasant to look upon in late summer when the apples turned bright red, but they were really sour, good mainly for pickles. Eve didn't know anything about apples, not having been around very long, so she picked one and took a bite. It was embarrassing to think of her and Adam running around naked.

That snake that talked Eve into swiping the apple? That puzzled me. A preacher explained that snakes were different back then, sort of charming. All the girls I knew were afraid of snakes, but Eve wasn't and neither was I.

The Garden of Eden was really neat. God took walks there to cool off. One day Adam and Eve heard him coming and they hid in the bushes because they were naked. They tried to cover up with leaves, which everyone knows won't work. God can see everything, even in the dark.

Where art thou, Adam? God called. He was really mad because Adam and Eve ate that apple. But he took pity and made them fur coats. One preacher said the first very first deaths were the animals God skinned to cover up Adam and Eve. There was a lesson there, I guess, but I kept thinking about the poor animals.

Then God kicked Adam and Eve out of the garden and made them pull weeds. He made the snake crawl on its belly forever and ever for tempting Eve. I guess the first snakes had legs, something like alligators. That snake was really Satan, so look out for him. He can show up all sorts of ways.

Then Adam and Eve began to begat and Cain and Able got born. My mother thought maybe they were twins, but I don't think so. My older sister Hazel was mean sometimes, but not all the time. Cain was really, really mean. He rose up one morning and slew his brother.

Everyone knows slewing is really bad, but Cain didn't care. When God caught up with him, he got plenty scared, thinking Abel's relatives might kill him.. Everyone was related back then. God put a mark on Cain to protect him. Some people thought God turned Cain black, but that couldn't be because later God turned Noah's grandson black. Some people said it was OK to make black people slaves because God said they would always be servants, but that comes later.

The flood! That was something else. Everyone got so evil God decided to start the world all over. He ordered Noah to build the ark because it was going to rain really hard and flood the whole world. The ark had to be big enough to hold Noah's family and every kind of creature on earth two by two, some seven by seven. Cows, horses, birds, chickens, lions. I wondered how Noah kept the lions from eating the chickens. Someone said up until then animals ate only vegetables, nuts, and hay; stuff like that. Meat eating came later.

Feeding all those animals from mice to elephants and the birds and snakes with only eight people must have taken all day. And think of the mess! You can't get girls to clean a barn. I remembered that from Grandma Preston's farm.

Noah kept working on the ark 120 years and his neighbors made fun of him because there was no water in the neighborhood except the Tigris and Euphrates Rivers which would never float a boat that big.

After he finished the ark, Noah loaded on all the animals and put his family on board and God shut the door. It started to rain and wouldn't quit. The water got higher and higher and the people pounded on the door but Noah wouldn't open it. All his neighbors drowned, which proves you can't fool around with God.

The rains came down and the floods came up until water covered the tallest mountains, wiping out every living thing on earth except maybe a few fish and bugs that can stand lots of water. The flood lasted most of a year.

Finally the ark got stuck on Mount Ararat. Just think of it! Floating all that time on its own and not drifting off to some strange country. Noah sent out birds to check out the land, but they flew to and fro and came back. Nowhere to land. Finally Noah sent out a dove and it came back with an olive leaf. That *really* bothered me. Every tree on earth would have died, being under water nearly a year. Where did the leaf come from? But that's what the Bible said, so you better believe it.

Everything had to start over. Animals, birds, plants, the whole works. Everything except Noah and his sons and their wives, and they had to get busy begetting, because Abraham was due to show up and Babylon and Egypt and Arabs with camels had to get started.

Another thing bothered me. First thing Noah did after the flood was get drunk. He took to his tent to sleep it off. Hot out, I guess. He slept naked. What bothered me was, with all plants killed by the flood, where did Noah find shoots to grow grapevines to grow grapes to make wine to get drunk on? My dad planted grape shoots along the chicken wire fence between our place and John Stai's old chicken coop and it took forever for grapes to show up. I guess Noah was a better farmer than my dad.

When Ham looked in the tent he saw his dad naked and Noah got really mad. He placed a curse on Ham; only the curse fell on Ham's son Canaan, which I didn't think was fair. Anyhow, Canaan turned black and moved to Africa, which is how Negroes got started.

Next, a bunch of men from Babel started building a tower to reach way up to heaven. God said enough of that. He mixed up their languages so they couldn't talk to each other. That is where Swedes came from—you can't understand them. Everyone had to find people they could talk to, and that's how nations got started. God had everything figured out.

Later on, Abraham moved in from Ur and God gave him the Promised Land, where the

Children of Israel got started. You see, Abraham begat Isaac and Isaac begat Jacob, and Jacob changed his name to Israel and begat a bunch of children, including Joseph.

One day Joseph's older brothers ganged up on him because they were jealous of the neat coat of many colors his dad made for him. They cast Joseph into a pit to die but changed their minds. They sold him to Arabs who had camels. The Arabs sold Joseph to Egypt, where he got thrown in jail. When he got out, he became the top guy in Egypt next to old Pharaoh. I liked that.

After a while, famine swept the land and all Joseph's relatives moved to Egypt and stayed there 400 years until Moses showed up to lead them back to the Promised Land.

After that things got really complicated, with judges and kings and captivities. But everything turned out all right because Jesus came and started Christmas. I'm sure glad he did.

The Story Tree

These stories came to light during an interim pastorate at Ironwood, Michigan. To lend flavor to my Sunday morning Kids' Time, I placed on the platform an eight-foot, leafless maple and called the story tree. I invited the kids to trim it with things God made.

Bird nests, a hornet nest, feathers, flowers, a wispy snake skin; they brought nature things. Each week I told a story; often about a tree trimming; sometime a story just for fun. I borrowed Son Joel's Cat in the Manger and dreamed up The Littlest Tree on the Mountain.

A sturdy willow shrub in the field next to the church caught my eye one spring Sunday as I drove into the parking lot. It boasted the biggest, whitest catkins I had ever seen. I knew I had to show the kids. At Kids' Time, I led a straggly line out the door and across the field to the willow. As the kids fingered the silk-soft catkins, a reckless impulse overpowered me. I said, "Next Sunday I'll tell you how the pussy willow got its mittens." I spent an anxious week waiting for the Muse to come, and here's what she brought:

How the Pussy Willow Got Its Mittens

A long time ago, a sturdy, proud willow lived on a hillside by the road that leads to the city. She had many, many children. This night, Mother Willow watched over her brood. How peacefully they slept. But soon she must wake them, and, as usual, they would be grumpy.

Other trees on the hillside stood like ghosts in the moonlight. Mother Willow sighed. Let the cedars reach for the sky; the oaks spread mighty limbs. She was content to be just a willow, the small tree that first welcomed spring.

Mother Willow understood trees, but she wondered about those strange creatures that passed by on the road. Now, well past midnight, two of them paused nearby. They were soldiers: one loud and tall, the other quiet and small. "Now we shall see what comes of that trouble-maker," said the tall one, sneering.

"He called himself a king," said the small one.

"A king? Well, he's a dead king now. Hail! King of the Ghosts!"

The small soldier peered about nervously. "They say he promised to return the third day. That would be today!"

"Don't be a fool! We've seen the last of that impostor. The dead are dead, forever dead."

"Then why did we seal his tomb? Why the guard?" The small man drew his cloak about him.

"You *are* a fool! What if his friends stole his body and claimed he was alive? What then?"

"Steal his body? Those pitiful men? They fled when we arrested him. And when he died, all but one watched from far off." The small man's voice grew hushed. "I tell you, as long as I live, I will never forget the day we killed Jesus."

Mother Willow stiffened. Killed Jesus? That kind, gentle man? How often he had walked by with his friends. How people talked of his wonders. Oh, how they talked about Lazarus! Why, only a week ago he rode by on a donkey with a great crowd waving palms and shouting Hosanna! Why would anyone want to kill Jesus?

The soldiers moved off into the fading darkness and Mother Willow exclaimed, "Well! If men are too dull to believe Jesus, I surely am not." Then a thought startled her: What if...? Children!" she cried, "Children! Wake up!"

"Oh Mother," groaned a small voice, "Just a little longer? No other trees are awake."

"Stir yourselves, Children. Jesus might pass this way, and if he does, we must be ready."

One by one the small willows stirred, stretching and shivering in the April chill. The smallest one whimpered, "It would be a great honor to greet Jesus, but I'm so very cold!"

"Oh dear," sighed Mother Willow. Quickly she gathered moonbeams and fine spider silk to spin the softest yarn. Her fingers flew as she knit tiny, silver mittens.

Warmed by their new mittens, the little willows stood waiting as dawn swept away the night. Suddenly, the smallest willow cried, "In the sky, over the city! Can those be angels?"

"Hush. Listen!" said big sister. A low rumble echoed across the valley. The earth trembled. "Mother, look!" whispered big sister, "*Someone is coming*!"

Mother Willow caught her breath. A lone figure approached. On tiptoe, the children watched. With one voice they cried, "It's him! It's him!" The little willows waved and waved, silver mittens catching the morning's first sun.

King Jesus paused. "Why, such a fine family. What lovely mittens! I wish I could stay but I must hurry to the garden; my friends will be looking for me." He smiled at Mother Willow. "Because your children were the first to welcome me back from the tomb, each spring I will give them new mittens to remind them I am alive."

And that's how the pussy willow got its mittens.

The Cat in the Manger
Joel Mattson

It was winter and Samson was cold, hungry and very, very tired. He meowed at the door, hoping only Jeremiah would hear. Jeremiah was Samson's friend but his fastidious wife Ruth was not. Again he meowed and the door opened a crack. Ruth's shrill voice sounded, "Jeremiah! Don't you *dare* let that cat in!" But Jeremiah hesitated just long enough for Samson to squeeze through.

He scooted toward the fireplace, hoping for a place to curl up and perhaps find a scrap left over from supper. But the inn was crowded. Guests had claimed all the good spots by the fire. As for food: not a morsel. Samson slipped quickly among the chairs, avoiding friendly hands. He didn't much like petting. Petters expected him to purr and Samson hadn't purred in long time.

Right now, food filled his mind. Looking cautiously about, he spotted the milk bucket in a far corner of the kitchen. Stealthily at first, then three quick bounds carried him to the bucket. He mounted it and began lapping greedily. "Jeremiah!" howled Ruth, "That cat's at the milk again!" Her broom swooshed and Samson ducked, knocking over the milk bucket. A second swoosh propelled him halfway to the front door, which Jeremiah had just opened to the knock of a traveler. "Stop that cat!" shrilled Ruth.

Fearing his wife's wrath more than offending a stranger, Jeremiah slammed the door. An agonized yowl caused him to jerk it open. Samson raced through the dark toward the stable, his tail flying at an odd angle. Skidding to a stop at the low door, he slipped inside and inspected his wounded tail. Man, the hurts! He licked the painful spot. "Broke again. Shoot! I won't be able to walk a fence for a week."

Hopping gingerly to the manger where he often slept, Samson burrowed in the musty hay to reflect on the night. A taste of fresh, sweet milk was the only bright spot. A broken tail was a small price to pay for such a treat. Then, voices.

Guarding his tail, Samson jumped to the earth floor and found a dark corner. An hour passed, then two. Samson snapped alert. Jeremiah stood near Joseph. Ruth hovered over Mary. A Cry!

Ever so gently, Ruth wrapped a tiny, wriggling baby in a soft blanket and laid him in Mary's arms. "That's about all we can do for now, my dear. The baby's just fine. Try to get some rest. I'll check on you in the morning."

As Jeremiah and Ruth slipped from the stable, she whispered, "I declare! Easiest birth I ever saw. That Mary! So calm! Her first, too. And most strange: before the child came she told me it would be a boy. Even called his name, Jesus. Now what kind of name is that for a country boy?"

Samson lay in the darkness, awed. "A baby, right here in my stable! I hope the little guy will be all right. People babies are so helpless. I better keep an eye on him.

Finally, Joseph placed the child in the manger and lay down by Mary. Samson crept silently forward, his tail aching. He sprang to the manger and saw the blanket had loosened, letting in the cold. The baby whimpered. This will never do, thought Samson. He nuzzled the child's face and a wee hand appeared above the blanket. Remembering from long ago his mother's comforting warmth, Samson turned, as cats will do, to prepare to lie near the baby. Samson snuggled close to share his warmth. Growing sleepy, he carefully drew his tail around him. It took a moment to sink in: the tail no longer ached! He flexed it. Not a twinge!

A deep purring mingled with the sleep sounds of guests and beasts. Outside, a bright star lit the cold, silent night. Samson drifted off, dreaming he heard angels singing.

The Littlest Tree on the Mountain

She was the littlest tree on the mountain and she knew it. Not only was she little, she was different. All around her tall cedars spread their magnificent branches. The littlest tree wished she could hide her crooked limbs and rough bark. She was a stranger. She didn't belong among cedars. The king's builders coveted their clear, fragrant wood. They wouldn't notice her.

All the cedars on the mountain dreamed they would one day see the king. The littlest tree often heard them boasting: "I will live in the king's palace!" said one. "Oh, I too," said another, looking proudly down his straight, sturdy trunk. "I will be a beam in the royal banquet hall. What grand sights I will see!" A huge cedar up the mountain boomed, "I will be a pillar in the throne room, the grandest place of all!" And a tall, slender cedar added, "I will be a mast on the king's fine ship and sail the Great Sea!"

The littlest tree looked down on her dark plain trunk. Oh, she was strong enough, and almost straight, but she was so small. She fought back tears. "I can never hope to see the king."

One autumn morning the woodcutters came. They laid down their axes and looked about. A

114

gruff voice called, "Over there. A fine tree for the king's ship." Axes rang and the slender cedar crashed to the ground. "There, that big one. Just right for the throne room. Take those smaller trees for the palace."

All day the woodcutters worked and the littlest tree grew sadder and sadder. "I will grow old and die on this mountain. I will never see the king." With all her might she wished she had never been born. In her sadness, she scarcely heard the gruff woodcutter say, "We need one more; it need not be big or fine. The Bethlehem innkeeper needs a small tree to repair his stable. There—that one will be just right."

The littlest tree cried as the axe bit her bark. "A stable! I'm fit only for a stable! Now for certain I will never see the king. What king would come to a stable?"

The Song of a Man and a Land

In 1958 our family moved from Muskegon, Michigan to serve Bethany Baptist in Anchorage, Alaska. The small congregation was blessed with gifted teens and college-agers.

Bethany became part of a cluster of churches, each with youths bursting with talent. Youth for Christ had died some years earlier, leaving the city without a broad youth fellowship. With far more zeal than wisdom, I set out to remedy that. I launched Anchorage Christian Youth (ACY).

Pastor Bill Heynen from the Christian Reformed Church, a skilled music man, put together a dynamite youth chorus. Blind Jimmie Trietch, Hammond Organ master, signed on. I rented the Sydney Lawrence Auditorium for nine Saturday nights September through May.

The monthly rallies drew a good attendance, and the energy and quality of the youth chorus impressed me. As Christmas approached, I phoned the major TV station and proposed a 30 minute holiday show, Christmas Cameos. The program director gave us a prime spot and the kids performed marvelously.

Then I proposed a Lincoln's birthday special called *The Song of a Man and a Land* with only the barest idea to go on. I worked on narrative verse to tie segments together. The 30-minute show drew accolades.

With too much on my plate, I quit TV productions, but the Lincoln theme kept percolating in my brain. Over several years, the three-page TV script evolved into the following sketch of our nation and our greatest president.

The Song of a Man and a Land

I am the nation that gave to the world
The man who is called Abe Lincoln.
I watched legend born in fire-lit books,
River rafts, the smooth shovel slate.
Quiet myth, gaunt truth,
The sad portrait speaks
Of Lincoln, Head of State.

Abe Lincoln and I are some alike,
A hybrid, a mingling of seeds.
The tall rebel man who freed other men
And the Nation most nearly free.
Note well this mingling of seeds in the land
That sent the tall man to his task,
Else tyrants will rule over slaves anew.
Even now some drink from death's flask.

Abe Lincoln's kind was not known in the world
When men first walked my valleys;
Not among my copper-skinned tribes
Nor the people of distant lands,
Where the rich were born to riches,
And the poor to servitude.

My people lived in shadowed days
With crude tools and simple ways.
Hogans and wigwams and mystic longhouses;
Shrill cries, soft chants,
The drums and the dance
To call men to war and to hunt.
I found no Lincoln among them.

Then, a west-blowing breeze
Brings to the lea
The sea-weary Santa Maria,
With a new kind of folk, milk-skinned and bold,
Who call my people *Indians*
They send more ships to probe my coasts,
To explore each river and bay.
They leave on my beach men, cargo and guns.
The ships sail eastward, away.
Red man stalks white man.
Death stalks them both.
I saw no wise man to guide them.

The white man came lusting for wealth,
His passion: power and treasure.
Before him I lay, a new world to gain,
But empire and gold was his pleasure.
He robbed my people,
They fought back and killed.
Red women trembled in wonder
That the sure arrow's whisper so soon was
hushed
By the musket's deadly thunder.

The Old World men unfurled gaudy flags
And plunged their staffs in my soil,
Claiming the land for England or France,
For Spain or Portugal.
This dull people dared to think
That man can own a land.
Dull indeed. Did they not know?
The land possesses man.
And this land claimed a man, Abe Lincoln.

Treasure and Empire, the hunger for fame,
Lured Old World men to me,
But another kind came with a Book and a song.
They spoke of a Man and a Tree.
They clung hard to life, but many died
Building homes where men could be free.
Free? Idle dream, Old World men,
Yet a seed of promise for me.

Freedom swelled in the heart
Of one Roger Williams,
And he thrust the seed deep in good soil.
In Rhode Island earth lay hope for new birth,
Ancestral seed for Abe Lincoln.

More nations sent their ships to my coasts
And spewed on my shores ten thousand.
I shuddered to see the plunder and waste
Of my creatures and their homeland.
Forests fled. Plows ripped the sod.
I saw my wild beauty fade
As timid hamlets grew bold,
Stretched their bounds to be cities,
Then spilled out the hardy beyond
My mountain defense
Toward the Great River.
Boone and more of his kind.

From the North Hampton pulpit
Of Jonathan Edwards
Rose a tide that swept down the land.
Wesley flint, Whitefield steel,
Gospel fire, God's command.

A light in the night of gospel decline
New seeds for the needs of mankind.
My soil spawned a hybrid, hardy and bold;
A blending of spirit and might;
Ideas more daring than men ever dreamed
Put British Redcoats to flight.
But the time was not right
For Abe Lincoln.

Then I opened my gates and the people poled
Their flatboats down the Ohio.
The rafts bore scant goods,
But their hearts bore great hope,
Nourished by seeds from Rhode Island.
Man's worth as a man, man's right to be free;
The stalk and the branch of that hybrid.

I watched the frontier push westward and north.
A man rode out on his circuit.
A thousand miles alone he rode
To marry and bury and comfort.
He fought demon rum, the Devil and greed.
His Bible, his prayer, his sermon;
More seed,
The leaf and the bud of the hybrid.

He summoned his flock
From the woodlands and fields;
They came, child and man, saint and sinner.
I swept clear the skies
That the great moon might rise
On the camp meeting
Hard by the river.

The tapping of feet to a staunch gospel beat;
Glory shouts rose to heaven, dulling the ear
To the chill cadence of fear
Already finding its rhythm.
My valleys caressed
And returned to the blest
In echo the song of the camp.
No lark sang so well as the music that fell
On the air in the night by the river.

A penitent wept at a hand-hewn bench,
Seeking peace with the price of tears.
Camp meeting seeds,
Swept by faith's breeze,
Added the worth to the hybrid.
The Cross and the Book,
And the man who found God,
Tore down the gross pride of high birth.
Freedom's cup filled,
Slowly filled, then spilled
To bathe the new Nation with might.
A land of the free! A home of the brave!
Almost.
Almost, but not quite.

A sore marred the health
Of the yet fledgling State,
A people come not by choice;
Bowed with a chain, dark children of pain,
They bore bitter seeds and a voice.
From the hold of foul ships;
Fettered, naked, for sale.
A cancer arose in my throng.

Their anguish-born prayer
From hearts torn with care,
Moses surely soon must come 'long!
Labor and suffer, weep and more toil,
Dark seeds of shame in my soil.

Now, three hundred years
Since the white man came
To mingle bloods in my land,
The seeds sown and grown,
And sown yet again
Swell. Nolen Creek,
Kentucky.
Tom Lincoln paces.
Nancy travails.
A cabin of logs hears the cry!
Moses? Aaron?
No, Abraham!
Tom could scarce lift his eye.
An uncomely babe, new-born Abe,
But a son! The darling of Nancy.

Now kings are born on palace beds,
Lords from the ranks of peerage.
Caesars inherit the toga of power,
The garland festooned brow;
Abe? Abe was a clod,
Born to the sod,
His hope lay in the plow.

Yet the soil Indiana then Illinois,
Betrayed a mystic rare fragrance.

The straw Abe chewed, the rail he hewed,
Nourished and wrought a wonder.
Abe jumped and wrestled, he swung his axe.
Abe listened and thought and read.
He learned of a Book left behind by poor Nancy.
No longer poor, now dead.
And the Clod caught the echo of dead Nancy's prayer
For her cabin-born, uncomely waif.
From the fruit of the seeds of three centuries
Prayer distilled a sweet wine of life.

Rough Abe drank deeply this nectar of God,
And allowed he was more than a clod.
The boy stood tall and became a man,
Taller than men around him.
He stood so tall he looked one day
To see the White House before him.

But it is not a hymn or camp meeting air
Or a mighty anthem I hear,
But a martial air, hot oratory,
The reticent marching of fear,
The retching of my child-State,
Sick with the gall of her slaves.
These are the sounds that fall on my ear
As Abe takes the President's chair.
Half slave half free?
Secede! Secede!
The boom of the guns of Fort Sumter.

I watched from a mountain my people at war;
Homes torn, lands ravaged, men fell.

I grew sick from the stench of Andersonville
And the northern dungeons of hell.
Spades tore my sod.
The weight of the dead!
Men hid their shame in my soil.

Then peace.
No, not peace,
War never brings peace
But a stupor before the next conflict.
Abe, tired, faced the task
Of mending his land,
But one shot was yet to be fired.
The last soldier to die
In that most tragic war
Was the man from the cabin of logs.

Death-felled,
Yet Abe Lincoln stood tall,
North and South lowered flags that day.
The Union reborn in hearts called to mourn,
They wore blue coats and gray.
A dirge from the South,
A moan from the mouth
Of the people Abe Lincoln set free.
Men gathered the Clod,
Turned back the sod,
My earth folded close.
Abe was gone.

From the north Arctic snow
To the summer green South

One flag, Abe's flag, was unfurled
To remember God's clod,
A new kind of man
In a new kind of land in the world.
A mingling of earth and faith and breath
Wrought by God for the dark and the fair,
From bold hybrid seeds
Of hymn tunes and creeds,
Of courage and daring and prayer.
In the Man, in the Land,
See the Book and the Cross.
Don't lose them.
Freedom lies there.

Part Three

Bits of Wisdom from Lloyd Mattson's Hole News
Compiled by Bob Kelly

Bob Kelly makes his home in Sun Lakes, Arizona. We connected through a mutual friend a few years back. Bob joined the Hole News gang and I signed on for his monthly KellyGram.

Bob's skill with words and his insights on writing immediately grabbed me. A world-class Quotemeister, he has compiled 1.7 million quotes, topically arranged in over 500 e-volumes. I never imagined he was gleaning thoughts from my scribbling's.

The Bits of Wisdom pages reached me at a critical juncture of my life. Word had gone out that Old Grandpa Lloyd was viewing Heaven on the near horizon. The prospect pleased me. I had lived long enough. I waited comfortably in the hospital, enjoying the outpouring of attention.

The arrival of Bob's quotes especially warmed me. A friend I greatly respected considered snippets from my writings worth preserving. I thought that a fine send-off. Turned out I didn't die. After long weeks of rehab, I returned home with a deepened commitment to make useful whatever days remained, including completing the final book of my memoir series.

The quotes Bob gathered summarize well how I view of life and faith as I continue the upward climb.

- A toolbox filled with screwdrivers is quite use-less when you need a pipe wrench.

- An honest memoir reports what God can do once we quit messing up.

- As the chill of the years steals on, seasoned friends warm us like an old sweater.

- Beware the bane of gospel jargon. We pack what we perceive to be truth into code words and phrases then wonder why outsiders don't get it. They are not rejecting the gospel; they haven't heard the gospel.

- Bible words are not amulets to drive off the devil. Satan can quote Scripture. The power of Scripture lies in its story, not in words cop-ied, translated, and interpreted over and over. The Bible's power lies in its truths burned in-to the heart by God's spirit. The Bible version makes little difference.

- Christian living must flow through all of life, not just our religion. Worship modes mean nothing by themselves. A store front is as fine a place to worship as a cathedral. Religion is a learned response, as much sociology as theology. Ritual may channel worship, but it is not the same as worship. God's grace flows from the risen Savior, channeled perhaps by priests, preachers, bishops, or ritual.

- Creator God is patient with his Earth and his people. We need patience too, but wearing smooth takes time.

- Do you think any Bible writer imagined they were jotting words that would last thousands of years? Translators tidied up inept writing; sometimes masked indelicate phrases. Few Bible authors were trained writers. I have no clue how inspiration worked, but I doubt God dictated the words.

- Everyone is a story. Our story may live but few years and touch only a few, but those few need to know what we have witnessed along the way. It's possible I have a chapter or two yet to write.

- Every friend enriches us. Friends are life's only real treasure. Gold won't hold your hand when you're crying or sit by your bed when you're dying. Gold can't add one nanosecond to your days and a shroud has no pockets. A friend is the only thing this life holds that you will find in heaven.

- Every sect and denomination is the long shadow of a leader with a theological axe to grind.

- Exploring scripture is invigorating; exploring dogmatically is deadly.

- Faith is an art not a science set in stone. We're all learners. We need to make space for each other.

- Given a little care, friends never wear out.

- Good memories, good friends, a measure of health, and knowing the Lord: the good life in old age. I am so blessed.

- Few of us will light the way for the masses yet each of us can light the way in our small corner. We may be the only light some folks have. But how about swapping our little light for a torch? A candle shines but a while then fades in a puddle of wax. A torch keeps burning and burning as long as you feed it fuel. A candle will light your way through the dark; a torch will light the way for others.

- Forget the big stuff; be alert for small opportunities; they are the big stuff.

- Forgiving ourselves may be the hardest forgiving we do. God knows all about us—no need reminding him. His grace is more than adequate. Get on with living Christ today; you will never run out of opportunities to serve.

- Friends around us care little about our theology. Jesus said we are light and salt and they don't need to talk to do their thing.

- Talent is a gift; we get no credit for talents. It's what we do with them that counts.

- God dwells among us; he will not be bound by our proof texts. He gives life to whoever will call on His name.

- God chose storytelling to communicate his message. We call God's story the Bible.

- God doesn't live in the church waiting for folks to show up. We bring him there with us.

- God doesn't quit working when we slow down. His promises may seem deferred, but they will never fail. I'll think on that when waiting times come.

- God gave two books and they know no conflict. The creation speaks of God's power, majesty, beauty, and order. The Bible speaks of God's care for mankind and his creation.

- God welcomes questions. His answers may surprise us.

- How I cling to my rights! The only right anyone has is the privilege of serving others. That's the gospel, the essence of Christianity.

- How poor we would be without books, those windows on the world of thought.

- Hugging holds more power than scolding.

- Human destiny rests with the sovereign grace of God, who is swayed neither by pamphlet nor professional muttering.

- I am convinced the Lord leaves us around as long as necessary to get done what he has in mind. Our job is to keep banging away.

- I can't do much about the flaws of far-flung humanity, but I can work on my flaws and perhaps ease some pain in my small circle.

- I don't understand geezers who are bored. Life picks up speed on the downhill side.

- A church is anywhere people gather in Jesus' name, even two or three. The location is not a factor.

- I like that verse, "Be still and know that I am God." We make too much noise.

- I like to think Creator God, who guides young hummingbirds and terns to places they have never been, led me to those places I could not have imagined in childhood. He still leads; where I care not. The path I leave to Him.

- I feed each day off heaven's treasure. I chatted this morning with Jesus; where Jesus is, 'tis heaven there. Jesus will be no more real in heaven than he is this moment.

- I love butterflies, God's flying flowers; so many variations, so ingeniously decorated.

- I spend no energy agonizing over God's will. As I walk with him, I am precisely where he wants me. When moving time comes, he will see to that. God manages the details; I just keep walking.

- If you walk with God, you get where He's going.

- To be useful in life, study Peter's fruitful life formula in 2 Peter 1:3-8. Sit a spell and study this seven-petaled flower: goodness, knowledge, self-control, perseverance, godliness, brotherly kindness, love. End results are guaranteed. There's not a religious function among them;

- If you're still climbing, you ain't over the hill.

- I'm growing long of tooth, but all who possess everlasting life are the same age. How good to dwell in the endless tomorrow.

- In Christ we become the best we can be (Ephesians 2:10), but note the closing words: "...created in Christ Jesus to do good works, *which God prepared in advance for us to do.*" God is not given to impulse. As his design for all creation unfolds, he works out his plan for each of his children, preparing and equipping them for every task he assigns. Mystery! All God's working is mystery.

- Jesus did not confine joy to religious stuff. He didn't go to church much. About every time he did, he got in trouble with the clergy.

- Jesus presented God's kingdom as relational, not religious.

- Jesus was a camper. He lived, taught, and prayed outdoors. He hiked wherever he went except twice.

- Live Christ: what does that mean? To find out, follow his steps; ponder his sayings. Go with him to the wedding party. Visit the woman at the well. Relive the stoning scene— shameless men and a shamed woman. Who walked off? Knock on Zacchaeus' door. Go fishing with the Four. Watch the Master in action and live like him. Have you noticed? He saved his harsh words for religious folks.

- Looking for a hobby? Collect friends. I guarantee their value will increase.

- Lord, as we touch lives, let us be neither spam nor junk mail. Stamp us with your person and presence.

- Love people where they are, as God does. Give them space.

- Most folks could not care less how we define inspiration, creation, or the millennium. They care how we live, how we treat them. Church folks spend too much time fighting each other; too little time fighting the hurt and darkness nearby.

- Never fear questioning your beliefs; you can't harm truth by doubting.

- Never let that which you can't control control you.

- No man's opinion determines truth.

- No sermon, however polished, is worth a hoot until it lodges in a heart.

- Old age either mellows or fossilizes. I choose mellow.

- Pay attention to God's truth. Those who live in harmony with God will live in harmony with one another.

- Pity the person who feels no awe when looking at life, the creation, and God's love for mankind.

- Prayer is adventure. If prayer bores you, it's your fault.

- Prayer was God's idea. Think of it! Creator God invites folks like us into his company.

- Rarely does anyone tell me they remember my sermons. Often people tell me they remember my stories. Doesn't take much to figure that out: quit sermonizing; tell stories.

- Religion puts us in a box with like-minded souls, and there are many boxes. Trouble begins when someone says, "My box is better than your box."

- Skeptics tell me I can't prove there's a God. Maybe not, but I'm sure enjoying Him.

- Spouting scripture is not witnessing. Witnesses are allowed to report only what they have seen and heard—ask any judge. The first thing a lawyer will attack is the witness' credibility. Credibility is where evangelism begins.

- The core essentials of our faith are God's sovereign grace and God's sovereign Son. What arrogance to think we have everything figured out.

- The cross is the meeting place for all children of the Kingdom, whatever name they bear.

- The good life in old age is the sum of its friends and memories.

- The gospel is what Jesus did for you and me not only to save us from hell someday but to spare us from the hell of self-living.

- The only legacy that matters is what you deposit in the hearts of others. That is the heart of the gospel.

- The only thing of intrinsic worth in all human experience is a friend.

- The sovereign grace of God: That's all we have; that's all there is. And that is mystery.

- The trouble with being a writer is, you're always writing. You write in your head then on the keyboard, and when you're onto something, writing just won't go away.

- The value of any book (or sermon) lies not in what it says but in what it causes the reader to think.

- Those who hold their viewpoint to be absolute, fixed truth will find their orthodoxy a jealous lover that brooks no competition.

- Time invested in family is money in the bank. I live day after day on riches from my investment.

- To live in constant thankfulness, tend to your memory board. Think what might have been!

- To those confined to a small pocket of the world I say, let your little light shine. It's dark in pockets.

- Want to be God's messenger? Live grace, love, and forgiveness. Someone is bound to get curious.

- Want to be rich in old age? Start collecting friends and memories.

- We depend utterly on God's sovereign grace. Someday he'll straighten out our kinks and clear up all mysteries.

- When we pray, we need not spell out details or remind the Lord to care. Prayer is simply God-awareness, a welling up of gratitude, a lingering over the needs of friends.

- We don't serve to be remembered.

-

- We have made Christianity way too complicated. We wring theology out of every detail, as though God planted a secret code within the narrative folks will miss if we don't tell them.

-

- We turn God into an institution when he wants to be our friend. All is of sovereign grace, and grace bears no labels.

- We need friends as much as we need food, shelter, and clothing. When you find yourself running low on fuel, plug into a friend. You'll get a real charge.

- We need to quit fussing over what we don't have and cultivate what God gave us, which is everything we need to fulfill his purpose.

- We serve a great God; his ways transcend our imagining. Relax and enjoy.

- What God has given us is always enough to fulfill his purpose for each moment. You can count on it.

- What the Lord has in mind will happen—the divine continuum. We who are involved have little idea what's really going on.

- When Christians become Christ-like the world will be more impressed. Jesus didn't say pure doctrine should mark us as his followers, but our pure love.

- You cannot be in tune with God and out of tune with people. It's in the Book.

- You cannot witness for Christ until you earn credibility, and that takes time.

Epilogue

Mystery and miracle: Those words pop up repeatedly as I think and write. Forces beyond knowing shape our days; events we can't account for carry us forward.

The Incarnation is the ultimate mystery/miracle. Apart from God Jesus, Christianity is but another religious-philosophical system. Compromise Jesus' oneness with the Father and Holy Spirit, and you destroy the faith once delivered to the saints. The 66-book anthology we call the Bible is subject to human tampering, but you can't tamper with Jesus, or use him. In him dwells the fullness of the Godhead bodily.

Growing old brings advantages as well as limitations. At 91, I am more content, fulfilled, and enthused about living that ever in my life. My friend list grows day by day; my must-read stack of books keeps mounting. I have looked down the valley and knew no fear. I have lost a step or two, but my brain shows little sign of wear. My favorite bit of wisdom from Bob Kelly's collection guides me: If you're still climbing, you ain't over the hill.

My Woodland Garden home is a miracle. I worked desperately hard to live elsewhere, but a woman was praying, "Lord, send me someone to talk to." She tends Woodland Garden's library, and I'm a book guy. Norma and I talk often.

A family group email I began when my Elsie was dying has grown into the Hole News blog with more than 300 subscribers from several lands. This book and eBooks in the works grew out of the Wordshed Mission, a retirement venture. Over 30,000 books have gone out, telling stories of God's work through unheralded servants of the kingdom.

Faith, friends, and memories: those are the riches of old age. My faith burns bright and memories still gather. As old friends leave for home, new friends fill the ranks. What lies ahead? I have no idea, nor do I care. I live by the olden rule: Walk with God, and you'll get where he's going.

Paul Boskoffsky, Aleut elder, is one old friend still banging away. He and Nattie endured the heartache of losing two of their grown children leaning on God's promise to supply all our needs according to his riches in Christ Jesus. Sometimes, supplying our needs calls for a miracle. Paul tells about that in his book, *Alaska: A Man from Kanatak:*

One year at the close of the camping season, I stayed behind to batten down the camp. The day was clear and breezy, ideal for flying, so after finishing my work I decided to cross the lake and check out the beach near the Gas Rocks for a possible camper overnight the next year. Flying campers over would save a long boat trip across the lake, which can get rough. My Super Cub was small, but it was great for beach landings.

I buzzed the beach and it looked fine. I landed smooth, but then I made a mistake: I forgot to raise the flaps before I turned the plane. The wind caught a wing and nosed me. I hit the switch, but not in time. The prop bit gravel.

I climbed out, pulled down the tail, and checked the prop. It was slightly bent. Now what! I was OK, but it was too far to walk out, and my family and friends would worry when I didn't get home. I knew search planes would never think to cross the lake. The only thing to do was try to fix the prop.

I always carry a tool kit, and after getting the prop off, I felt I could straighten it with the right tool. But the hand axe from my tool kit was too light. OK. Find a large rock.

For two hours I walked the beach in both directions and found only small stones tumbled smooth by the surf. It was a real predicament. I grew desperate. I prayed out loud, "Lord, please help me!"

As I walked toward the plane thinking what to do, I saw an old stick poking up from the tundra at the edge of the beach. I pulled on it—I don't know why—and to my amazement, on the other end of the stick was a geologist's hammer. I lifted it high and shouted, "Thank you Lord!"

The hammer was just right. I made a bed in the sand, worked gently on the prop, eyeballed it, and put it back on the plane. Nervously, I cranked the engine. It fired and ran smooth! I flew home rejoicing.

I still have the prop, and I keep the miracle hammer on my bookcase to remind me of God's love and provision for His people. He put the hammer at just the right place, waiting for me. It had been there long years, swept by many storms. The handle was nearly rotted off.

People ask how a hammer like that could have got to such an out of the way place. I can only guess, but many years ago oil prospectors explored that region. Perhaps a prospector lost his hammer. He sure picked a handy place to lose it!

I was reminded of the Bible story about Elisha and the man who lost an axe head in the Jordan River. Axes were precious in those days. Look up 2 Kings 6:6-7 to learn how the prophet got the axe head back. I wrote that text on my hammer. God still works miracles.